Nicole has the ability to enter tough places and connect us to light and hope. Thanks, Nicole, for doing it again.

—Dr. Henry Cloud, author, *Power of the Other*

Nicole is unbelievably funny, incredibly familiar with her own unconscious (and everybody else's), and has the rare talent of making you want to read every word she writes. It's unusual to find this kind of wit with this much brilliant psychological insight.

—Dr. Neil Clark Warren, founder, eHarmony.com

I love the promise of this book. We are all familiar with the crazy pace of life. What a gift to be guided to the calm.

—Sheila Walsh, author, *In the Middle of the Mess*

Nicole deftly reveals what brokenness looks and feels like, and with humor and vulnerability, invites us to walk with her through the necessary, painful, and ultimately liberating steps toward wholeness and joy. If a truly more integrated life is what you are looking for, this is the place to start.

—Curt Thompson, MD

In her new book, my dear friend Nicole bravely shares her journey, draws a map we can use, and hands us the keys. If you've ever thought something has to change in your crazy life, this book will be your guide.

—Angela Thomas Pharr, speaker; bestselling author, *Redeemed*

Nicole is not only one of the best communicators we know, she's also one of the most winsome and wise friends we have. Witnessing her journey has profoundly changed our lives, and this book will no doubt change yours too.

—Jay and Katherine Wolf, coauthors
and cofounders of Hope Heals

With unusual candor, humor, and insight, Nicole shows women how to experience inner peace, joy, and sanity in the "center of their crazy." She offers practical tools for finding calm and thriving amid a chaotic schedule, home life, and career.

—Doree Donaldson, director, Convoy: Women

In a world wrought by distraction and busyness, Nicole offers an easy to follow pathway that will lead you to a more focused and calm life. No matter what your life looks like now, it will be enriched by the reading of these pages.

—Pepper Sweeney, actor and director

During the first few pages of Nicole's book, you will laugh knowingly and look around sheepishly. Then she will take you on a journey to recover your own soul. Her book is a gift.

—Laurie Polich Short, author, When Changing
Nothing Changes Everything

CREATING

Calm

IN THE CENTER OF

Crazy

CREATING

Calm

IN THE CENTER OF

Crazy

MAKING ROOM FOR YOUR SOUL
IN AN OVERCROWDED LIFE

NICOLE JOHNSON

ZONDERVAN®

ZONDERVAN

Creating Calm in the Center of Crazy
Copyright © 2017 by Nicole Johnson

Requests for information should be addressed to:
Zondervan, *3900 Sparks Dr. SE, Grand Rapids, Michigan 49546*

Library of Congress Cataloging-in-Publication Data

ISBN 978-0-310-34507-7 (hardcover)

ISBN 978-0-310-34508-4 (ebook)

Cover art: Corrie Lauridsen
Interior design: Denise Froehlich

First printing April 2017 / Printed in the United States of America

For the Seasons Weekend community;

without you there would be no story

Contents

THE PERFECTION GARDEN

If I could plant a Perfection Garden
I'd grow a lot of peaceful parsley to stop the meanness
in the world.
It's a tall beautiful purple plant that calms people down!
When you eat it, it changes frowns into smiles.
My mom would plant the Time Thyme.
She always needs more time to take care of our family!
Time Thyme is amazing!
When you eat it, it makes the clock go backwards for
two hours
So my mom can get more done!

—MY SON, ELLIOT, AGE 7, 2013

THIS BOOK was nine years in the making.

I tell you this not to raise your expectations but to lower them. It has taken me that long to get enough space and calm in my life to write this book.

My recipe for crazy is not one I would recommend, but most of us have the ingredients on hand—busy work schedule; relationships and responsibilities that don't respond to our timetable; full social calendar; parenting activities; and so on. Depending on the mix and the amount of each ingredient, we create crazy or we create calm.

Of course, no one sets out to create crazy. I certainly didn't. Crazy is what happened to me when I was too overwhelmed to pay attention to my life. After my two babies were born in the midst of my full-time touring schedule, I wasn't paying attention to my name, much less whether I was living a meaningful life. I was in survival mode and so grateful we were all still alive at the end of each day!

At the time I'm writing this, I have not cracked the

code to having a completely sane and calm life. I'm not sure there is such a thing. It's more like one day my heart and soul were cracked open through a crisis. Forced by emotional pain to sit still, I discovered a deeper place inside myself, partly by accident and partly by choosing to remain still in the midst of the pain. Resisting the pull to return to crazy, I discovered some new ways to create calm amid a life that too often floods its banks.

So if you bought this book thinking I have all the answers you need to create calm, don't feel bad for asking for your money back. I am not living on a serene island, enjoying umbrella drinks and having spa treatments.

When I started this book, it was about ways a person could have a calmer life. I was several chapters in, feeling great about what I was writing, when it dawned on me that I wasn't sharing the whole story. I think subconsciously I was avoiding the awful truth: a crisis was the catalyst for creating calm. Suddenly, I wasn't as keen on writing this book. I feared the emotional effort involved to write *that* book would take way more time and explanation than I had in me. *You're trying to help people find calm, for crying out loud! Why make yourself crazy trying to write about something so difficult and so intensely personal? Why not just journal about it and look back on it privately as needed? Better still, why not pick another subject altogether, like Seven Simple Meals for Busy Families? Surely that will create calm somewhere in the world!*

I had to ask myself whether writing such a personal book about creating calm would warrant the added crazy (walking through the crisis again, spending more time writing than I'd anticipated, having less freedom to enjoy the open space I'd created, putting more pressure on my husband) that this kind of writing requires of me. I wasn't sure. I'm still not sure. (Don't ask my kids whether it was warranted—unless you can wait a few more years.) Either way, I committed to restart the book and share more about what started me on the journey, not just the benefits that I have experienced since. This became a better book and I became a better student of myself and of the world around me. A world, I firmly believe needs more voices willing to examine the crazy way we live these days. With overcommitted schedules, pressure-filled homes, mad racing about, and way too much wine drinking (but enough about my life), this "crazy" way of our culture is not healthy, nor does it seem deeply satisfying to anyone. Not only does it not produce what we have been led to think it will, this insanely busy living is stealing from the marrow of our souls the very richness we need to create meaningful lives.

I wish I could promise that simply reading this book will create a center of calm in your life. But nothing of great value has ever come to me without hard work. I don't know where I got the idea that it should, but I'm guessing it came from writers who didn't share the full story in their writings. People who wanted to make hard things look easy so people like me would buy their books and they could move to a serene island and enjoy umbrella drinks and spa treatments.

I hope that in sharing the truth of my unconventional path in this personal way, those who long for something more will know that while it isn't easy, it is indeed possible. You really can stop. You really can create calm in the center of crazy. But I also want to say to those who consistently live with a high level of pressure and craziness because they enjoy it or think it doesn't really matter: Believe me, it matters. Slow down, and do it now while you still have something worth slowing down for. You won't regret it. That I can promise you.

PART 1

My Journey out of Crazy

CHAPTER 1

Crazy

"PAIN IS THE MEGAPHONE God uses to rouse a deaf world," wrote C. S. Lewis in *The Problem of Pain*.[1] I wouldn't have said I was deaf, but pain was the megaphone that halted my crazy world. Pain brings life screeching to a halt, sometimes for days or months, and sometimes just for a moment. Fortunately a moment is all it takes.

In the spring of 2012, I experienced a crisis. Not in my marriage, not with my children, but in a long-standing, cherished friendship. Since it happened, I have tried to put many words on this experience in an attempt to make sense of it, but I've been unable to. I can, however, describe the way this pain felt. It was as though:

- my heart was the *Titanic* and I'd hit an iceberg that ripped through my hull.
- my heart was a tomato that got dropped from the top of the Empire State Building.
- my heart was a box of china that got backed over by a Mack truck, three times.

I'm sure your mind wants details; I get that. We think we need all the information in order to make sense of things, but we're wrong. Sometimes all the details in the world can't make the pain we feel make sense because the "why" still eludes us. Such was the case for me. I'll spare you the specifics and ask you to trust me that the details don't matter. For some reason, unknown to me, a friend of fifteen years rejected me. Closed the door to discussion and locked it from her side. No matter how many times I tried to make sense of it, I couldn't. And like the *Titanic* steaming along in the night, I never saw the iceberg coming.

Here is what I know now: when everything hits the ground or the fan or whatever metaphor we use to describe it, if it's happened to you, the details quickly fade as the awful enters the picture and changes life forever.

When the phone call comes, when the doorbell rings, when the letter arrives, when the doctor says

_____, we cannot recall the specifics. We condense the memory of what happened to "the day life fell apart."

MY RECIPE FOR CRAZY

In the years leading up to this crisis, I'd been in a long stretch of crazy. I call it crazy because that's the term I picked up from our culture when the busyness of life goes past busy. When busy redlines, we call it crazy busy. Some call it insanely busy. I have used those very words to describe my life to others. It didn't seem like hyperbole, because it wasn't. Life was out of control. That's not crazy busy, that's just plain crazy.

I got there honestly. This long stretch of crazy began for the very best of reasons. Complete, heart-stopping, soul-throbbing, mind-numbing love that engulfed my being the day my first child was born. I was baptized in it again when my second one arrived. The happy immersion that had me swimming in the deep end of love the first few years turned into a fear of drowning when I felt I couldn't come up for air. Here are the CliffsNotes of the last ten years:

I was on tour full-time as a dramatist with Women of Faith, a Christian women's conference, from 1999 to 2011. In 2003, I met Roy. We married in 2005. Our son, Elliot, was born in 2007; our daughter, Abigail, was born in 2009. Even though I'd already reduced my travel schedule, cutting back from twenty-eight weekends to fifteen, life on the road with kids was not easy to manage. It wasn't what we saw for the future of our little family, the family we'd waited so long for and felt so grateful to have. Because of our desire for something more than hotel kids' menus and dressing room play areas, as well as some changes in Women of Faith, I retired in 2011. Elliot was in preschool, Abigail was two, and Roy and I were learning a new way of life. Raising little ones in our forties brought an alternate reality that we'd never imagined or prepared for when we dreamed of starting a family.

While I had retired from the kind of touring that required me to be gone from home fifteen weekends a year, I still wanted to continue performing and writing. I decided this was the opportunity to pursue the direction that had been simmering on the back burner for a few years. I envisioned creating a weekend experience for people like me—people who are tired, overwhelmed, partly burned out, slightly cynical, and more than a little leery of weekend experiences. I longed to see an intimate gathering that focused on getting still and learning to rest in the presence of God in every season of life. I decided to name it Seasons Weekend and hold it four times a year.

While I wanted to create this weekend for people like me, I had no idea how much I needed it myself. Had I been standing outside my life in 2012 and watching it unfold, this is what I would be witnessing: a distracted, overcommitted, multitasking wife and mother too often comparing herself with others, living under enormous pressure to do meaningful work—all to create a wonderful life.

Again, I trust I ended up in crazy with the best of intentions. But only hindsight holds perfect clarity, and I can see now that what began in the cozy, warm water of motherhood slowly, and without my awareness or consent, became the boiling water of a pressure cooker.

There were five main ingredients in the recipe that created crazy in my life.

1. Distraction

In some strange twist of fate, distraction, ever the enemy of my grown-up mind, became something to embrace, even celebrate, when I had kids. Many parenting experts agree that in the middle of a major meltdown in the grocery store, church, or public bathroom stall, distracting a child from what's bugging them pays great dividends.

I confess, this was a foreign concept to me at first. I don't like being distracted or distracting others, especially on purpose. I wasn't sure distracting my kids when they were upset was the right thing to do. I wasn't even sure I could do it. Turns out, I could do it and do it well.

"No, we can't take Charlie's favorite stuffed platypus home with us, but quick, look over here! Mommy is standing on her head for you!"

"I know we didn't bring your favorite DVD, but look at this! A wallet. See, it has compartments and cards. Okay, sure, it tastes good too." Who cares if it's Louis Vuitton? Chew away, tear it apart.

"I know you can't talk yet and that you don't understand this, but if you'll stop crying, I'll buy you a horse."

Authenticity took a back seat to circus acts and magic tricks. Motherhood makes multiple personalities look normal and necessary. *Crazy* is a very suitable adjective. Of course, I had never previously loved anything enough to allow it to drag me around like a wheeled pull-toy, so I was learning crazy and was happy as a clam.

I was learning (in important ways) how to lay down many of my task-oriented, focused ways and just be with my children without an agenda or even a complete thought. What I didn't realize was how hard it might be later to hone my work skills back into something sharp enough to cut more than a grilled-cheese sandwich. But I'm getting ahead of myself.

2. Overcommitment

My propensity to overcommit didn't start with children, but preschool brought it out of remission. I'd been so protective of my time with the little ones and so discouraged by my inability to shower regularly that I became much more of a homebody than I'd ever been in my life—until preschool hit. Then my preexisting condition came roaring back.

"We are a very hands-on, parent-involved school," we heard on the tour. They weren't kidding. I think many of the other mothers were coming out of their nests too, and we all were breathing the heady air of newfound freedom from 9:00 a.m. to 12:00 p.m. I tried to pack as much into those three hours as humanly possible. I had to work out, catch up on email, pay the bills, and spend special time with Abigail. I forgot all I had learned about meander and went straight to sprint.

When Elliot entered preschool, I dived in, wanting to be hands-on and involved, but also (and this one was new to me) wanting to demonstrate my commitment alongside other mothers. I heard what was said about the ones who weren't "involved." I saw the praise heaped upon the parents who consistently volunteered to do construction projects and clean-up days. There were too many activities to be hands-on for, and I didn't have enough hands! What kind of mother could miss the pancake breakfast? There were so many things to create; we *need* your help; please work to build the mosaic on the wall as your class legacy to the school! Be sure to sign up for pajama night on Friday. And don't forget to bring the snacks when it's your family's turn!

I really had learned to say no in my other life. I had learned, at least well enough, to make my commitment level match my availability. But I wasn't Nicole Johnson anymore; I was *Elliot's mom*. What would they say about *Elliot's mom* if she wasn't committed enough? "Poor Elliot, his mother doesn't volunteer very much. Bless her heart, she must have to work a lot to afford this preschool." This kind of thinking got me in real trouble.

Then along comes Abigail, heading to the same school. I can't back off from what I did for Elliot or it would be "poor Abigail." Not to mention by this time Elliot has started kindergarten, thrusting me into a new circle of parents who will be trying to decide what they think about Elliot's mom. Such a trap, then and now. Always.

I was also juggling the commitments and responsibilities that came with work. None of these things were bad or wrong. These are good things, but I still had a marriage to maintain, two kids in school with different demands, neighbors to love, aging parents to care for, church involvement, birthday parties to attend and throw, music lessons to practice, craft projects to make, holidays to plan, and vacations to enjoy. I wasn't enjoying much of anything. I was losing the capacity for real enjoyment.

3. Multitasking

Multitasking is the engine that drives overcommitment because it creates the illusion that we can successfully handle multiple tasks simultaneously as well as switch quickly from one task to another. I really believe women invented this word with their actions, while men talked about it as a new emphasis at work, where they were learning to talk on the phone *and* write something down! This is one area where we women really outshine our male counterparts, perhaps because we've been required to multitask since the beginning of time. It was an early survival skill to be able to hold the baby while cooking a meal over the fire and chasing away wild animals! Fortunately, these skills still serve us well, whether at home with kids or coordinating the endless tasks of modern life.

Women are good at multitasking, period. I'm good at it. I multitask as a way of life. There are days when I think it might be my greatest talent. I can wrap a present and write the birthday card for a party, get a snack for one child, pour a glass of milk for another, check the caller ID when the phone rings, find the email with the address for the party, and have time to pat myself on the back for having remembered to get fuel in the minivan the day before! This is right about the time my husband yells from another room, "Do we have a birthday party to go to today?" I smile at what others before me have called job security.

About fifteen years ago, I wrote a comedic vignette on multitasking called *Hats!* It portrays about ten different hats that women wear on any given day, at the drop of a hat, pun intended. From the mom hat to the chauffer hat, to the chef hat to the psychologist hat, we are hilarious multitasking maniacs.

But recently neurologists have discovered that what multitasking is doing to our brains is not so hilarious. Turns out *multitasking* may be the worst word invented in the twenty-first century, basically because while our brains can sometimes function like computers, they are not computers. When we multitask, we become less effective at everything. We become faster at doing certain things, but slower at accomplishing anything.

Multitasking is often a clever and inoffensive euphemism for not paying attention. If I am in the middle of ten different things, surely I can't be held accountable if I'm not giving you my full attention. I can think of many times I've dialed the wrong number because I was in the middle of writing a note to one of my kids' teachers at the same time. I count many instances when I've sent an email to the wrong recipient because my computer autofilled the wrong name, and because I wasn't paying attention, I didn't even notice it. I've woken up with multitasking hangovers, having agreed to something the kids were asking me for that I didn't intend to agree to, but they caught me in the middle of doing three things at once and took advantage of my distractedness. All the devices designed to help me multitask are limited by one flawed, rushed woman who is trying to do too much at one time.

Looking back I can see so clearly how multitasking contributed to the feeling that I was drowning in the middle of my own life. I was doing more stuff than ever yet getting less done. I was working harder than ever but having much less to show for it. Multitasking led me to feel productive when actually it was keeping me from real and meaningful productivity. Which only meant that soon I was going to feel more overwhelmed, and that I'd have to try even harder to feel a sense of accomplishment. Multitasking was increasing the speed of the very treadmill I was trying to get off.

So was comparison.

4. Comparison

There was a span of about a year and half after Abigail was born that I was so mentally and emotionally fatigued from the strain of sleep deprivation and volcanic spit-up, I would have had to guess my name. And I wouldn't have cared if I got it wrong—it didn't matter anyway. I couldn't tell you about current events and couldn't remember past ones. I think I went three years without seeing a movie in the theater—maybe longer, who knows? This came with a great deal of shame for me as others discussed what movies were good and what they had seen. I remember thinking, *How do you even get out of the house? Why is motherhood so hard for me? Women have done this before. For millennia, actually. I'm certainly not the first woman over forty to have two kids. I should be able to do this. Other moms are doing it, and doing it well. What is wrong with me?*

As women, it seems we come out of the womb comparing ourselves with those around us. We compare everything—houses, husbands, rear ends, clothes, toys—you name it and we can tell you who has a better one than we do. We compare our lives, our gifts, and even our struggles.

If we used comparison to help us recognize some of our negatives and then we made positive changes, this would be effective. But we don't stop there. We take our comparisons and use them as measuring sticks for our worth. When we compare ourselves with others and we believe we come out favorably, we gain a false sense of pride. This can lead to smug and judgmental behavior. When we compare ourselves with others we deem better or at least better in a certain category, like the house she lives in, we place our own score in the minus category. I don't even think we're fully aware of how often we rank ourselves in light of others.

This kind of comparison creates shame, an ungrateful heart, bitterness, and envy; I know this firsthand. Comparison is the evil twin of contentment. It is the thief of gratitude, and it sneaks into my heart and robs me so blind that I can no longer see or appreciate all that I have and all that I am truly capable of. Comparison opens wide the front door and invites crazy to sit at my kitchen table.

When I glance at the magazine rack while in line at the grocery, I end up on the rack of comparison. I start to think to myself, *I don't look like that in my small sparkly dress. Why, I don't even have a small sparkly dress. I don't have a small, sparkly anything,* and something inside me crumbles: my gratitude for the enormous amount I do have.

Shame can also enter the picture when we compare our struggles. Again, because I choose to compare myself with those who I think are doing it better, I feel shame when I struggle with something I perceive other women don't struggle with. If something is hard for me and I see it comes easily to you, I can feel badly that I struggle at all. But isn't it possible that there is something for me to learn by struggling? Perhaps this is a vital piece of my journey that I would miss if I didn't struggle. Comparison never reveals the whole story, only as much of the story as we need to feel inferior. It's hard to admit, but we are doing this to ourselves.

Comparison creates emotional craziness. It uses the things we see around us to whisper our worst fears to our souls: *You're not good enough. You're not a good mother. You're not smart enough. You're not pretty enough. You're not whatever enough.* You fill in the blank with what your comparison tells you. It's important to know what it says, if only so you can know that this is not the voice of love. This is not the voice to listen to. But when I found myself distracted and overcommitted and multitasking on the treadmill of performance, it was the loudest voice I heard. *Keep going! Run harder! If you stop, everything will come crashing down.* This leads to enormous pressure to keep it all together.

5. Pressure

I think I'm pretty good at managing a busy life. I'm a star performer at getting things done. I am good at crossing stuff off my list. I think I have an excellent reputation for being a go-to person for accomplishing things. I wouldn't want to trade this (the good part, not the prideful part), but coupled with my propensity to overcommit, I create the perfect environment for pressure. Given a choice, I frequently choose high-pressure intensity over low-pressure calm, and I'm not sure why. Some women are slow cookers. Like Crock-Pots, they take a long time to heat up and everything cooks at a very low temperature all day. While I like to think like a slow cooker, I mostly work like a pressure cooker.

Here's how pressure cookers work. When liquid inside the pot boils, the liquid is trapped inside the pot. Having no release, the steam builds up pressure. The pressure of the trapped steam creates the PSI (pounds per square inch) that makes pressure cookers do their work in a fraction of the time it takes conventional methods. But if for some reason the pressure inside the cooker doesn't shut off, the contents will no longer be recognizable as food.

When it comes to too much pressure, our lives don't fare much better.

Beginnings of any sort are stressful and pressure filled. Starting anything new—working a new job, kids attending a new school, moving to a new city or even into a new home—there is always more work to do than we anticipated, and it always costs more than we'd planned to pay. There is a learning curve, and even if we crest the curve, it sends us careening downhill faster than Shaun White on the half-pipe. Such was the case for me in starting Seasons Weekend, the nonprofit I mentioned earlier. I was no longer earning income, and the cost of this endeavor was more than I imagined. I took a very big risk and used my retirement savings to get the weekend off the ground, fully believing I'd be able to put that money back in once Seasons was up and running. (I do not recommend this, by the way.) The pressure was enormous, not only for me but for my family as well. There was too much steam trapped inside the pot! The pressure per square inch in my household was dangerously high, with no relief in sight.

I've heard it said that stress doesn't come from what you're doing; it comes from what you think you *should* be doing. So when you should be working on a project or when you should be making money by now in your new company, or when you should be creating more family memories and you're *not* doing those things, it generates pressure and stress.

My point is this: when we have a lot of responsibility and are expected to be holding everything together, because we are women and that is exactly what we do, we put too much pressure on ourselves. Because we've consistently done too much—and done it well—we are expected to keep up that level of accomplishment. We try to make it look effortless. We would never want anyone to feel bad that we have to work so hard, so we keep buying the birthday presents for all the parties the kids are invited to; we keep picking up the gluten-free, sugar-free, dairy-free cookies for the bake sale; we keep making sure homework gets done; we keep the family attending church activities; we keep calling Mom, not as often as she would like, but as regularly as we can; we keep working extra hours; we keep paying bills, finding socks, driving carpool, changing light bulbs . . . *Mayday! Mayday! She's gonna blow!*

No one can say ahead of time how much pressure

she can handle. The only way a person can really find out is by getting it wrong, by taking on more than she can handle. But that is dangerous. What could be worse than turning everything inside my pressure-filled life into mush? And only because I discovered I couldn't manage as much pressure as I thought I could? Too costly.

I laugh at the thought of putting this on my tombstone: "I almost got it all done!"

NOT A PRETTY PICTURE

That, my friends, is how I got to such a high level of crazy in my life. I'm sure you can see the way these ingredients connect to each other and feed off each other. Multitasking leads to distraction, comparison leads to overcommitment, overcommitment creates pressure that needs to be relieved by distraction, and so on and so on. Round and round and round it goes, and where it stops, nobody knows, because it doesn't stop. I had to stop it.

My life was forever changed with the birth of my children, and over the years, the sweet warmth of family love has only grown and intensified. But looking back, I can see the ways I was inviting crazy and all that inevitably came through the door with it. I had no idea there was any other way. I feel fortunate that we did survive living under that much pressure and that nothing exploded that couldn't be repaired or wiped off the walls, but I would never do it that way again.

Sometimes I close my eyes and picture those days. I can clearly see myself running around like crazy, distracted, overcommitted, constantly multitasking, and way too often comparing myself with others and coming up short. I put too much pressure on myself. I thought I should be able to do it all, handle it all, and love every minute of it. It was so unfair of me to do this to myself, and I can cry just thinking about it.

No woman likes looking at unflattering pictures of herself, let alone showing those pictures to others. But to rip up these photos and forget about them would be to waste what they have taught me. It's not that I was a bad person during this time or that terrible events were happening. I loved my husband and children, created memories that will last a lifetime, and did meaningful work. But I never stopped long enough to identify the crazy in these pictures of myself, and honestly if I had seen the crazy, I don't think I would have recognized it as crazy at the time. I'd gotten caught up in my desire to get it all done, make everyone happy, keep the plates spinning, and look good while doing it. But I was distracted, and at times distraught, as I kept looking to the left and to the right and seeing others I thought were doing it better.

Something had to give. I just never imagined *everything* would have to give. I had no idea my heart would have to shatter into a million pieces to show me how to be whole again. Or how a miserable and horrible crash could end up being the very thing I needed to stop the crazy train. Or that this crisis could do something for me I never would have been able to do for myself.

CHAPTER 2

Crisis

IT WAS LATE IN THE AFTERNOON and I was flying home from a speaking engagement. I had an hour or so between flights and I grabbed a sandwich and began to check my email. I wish to this day I had simply waited until I got home to "check in." As I scrolled through my inbox, I happened to open the one with the bomb in it. Reading that email ushered in The Day Life Fell Apart.

I can see myself sitting in the food court near the K Gates at O'Hare, and I can tell you what I was wearing and the ingredients of the sandwich I was eating, but as I write these words almost four years later, I cannot tell you why my friend sent that email. I was not granted the "why" piece and was left in the dark to feel around for remaining pieces of what might be left after the explosion. I couldn't find much.

Pain may well be life's best teacher if we are willing students. Pain creates an immediate and intense awareness when it strikes, followed by very focused attention on the area of the pain. In the night, if I need to get up for some reason, I'm not thinking about my toes. But when I smash my little piggy on the leg of the coffee table, I am instantly aware of that baby toe on the end. When I got up to get water, my brain wasn't making me aware of my toes. But after the smash, my attention went straight to my toe and to not screaming.

In the same way, I'm quite sure I had a heart and soul before The Day Life Fell Apart, but I wasn't aware of them in the way I soon would be. As far as I knew, they were working together well. But when the bomb in my inbox exploded, my attention instantly focused on my heart and on not screaming. The pain was searing and hot; I could have just slumped over onto the floor. People would have assumed I'd had a heart attack; I would have been okay with that. Going to the ER would have given me some space to fall apart unashamedly, but as it went, I had to hold it together enough to throw away an uneaten sandwich, show my boarding pass to the gate agent, put my stuff in the overhead bin, and sit down in 22E before I could turn toward the window and sob.

I would like to tell you that it doesn't necessarily take a crisis to wake you up, but it did for me. I remember a comedian making fun of the saying, "Guns don't kill people; people kill people," by adding, "This could be true, but let's just say, a gun *really* helps!"

I would never wish a crisis on anyone, but if you're in the middle of a catastrophe, don't let it go to waste. It will open you up and refocus your attention on your heart and your life. Don't think, *I'll get through this crisis and then figure out how to live a better life on the other side.* Your crisis can lead you to the better life. Every crisis has an offering in the midst of the awful. It's redemption for the suffering.

All is not lost if you're not in a crisis. In fact, give thanks and maybe pick up this book again later. Or maybe just hang out for a bit, because like good surfers waiting for the next big wave, it's possible a crisis is coming soon.

I can think of two reasons it took something like that exploding email to change my direction and ultimately the course of my life:

1. Simply wanting change was not enough to bring about the change I wanted.

2. It took a perspective-altering event for me to see how crazy life had become.

WHY WANTING CHANGE IS NOT ENOUGH

I had been aware for years that my life was crazy. I found myself thinking regularly that I wanted to be living a different way long before The Day Life Fell Apart. I wasn't alone in this. I have found parents at my children's school, neighbors on my street, and women I talk to at events who also know life is too crazy. They say things like, "This is insane," or, "I can't keep living this way," but six months later, nothing has changed. Wanting life to settle down or change never results in actual change because "want to" is not strong enough to make it happen.

If the knowledge that life is crazy could make our lives calm, we would all be living differently by now. The magazines that fill every rack in the grocery store promise that yes, we too can organize and simplify our lives. Look how easy it is with these simple steps. We buy the magazine, read the steps—and nothing changes. The harsh reality is that information alone does not bring about change. I've been a subscriber to *Real Simple* magazine for ten years and my life is not one bit simpler because of it. In fact, the subscription itself adds pressure with every issue. How will I ever be able to simplify my life if I can't even find the time to read *Real Simple*? It's real simple; we don't change unless we have to.

If knowing that smoking will kill you could make someone stop, no one would smoke. But people can read study after study about smoking and its negative effects on the heart and lungs and even on a child in the womb, and still they continue smoking. Often it is not until the crisis of cancer hits or the pregnancy test is positive that real and lasting change becomes possible.

Think about recent studies on cortisol levels in our bodies. Research proves that stress takes a toll on us physically.[2] We *know* this, yet we continue to live with dangerously high stress levels, naively hoping and praying it doesn't take its toll on *us*. Knowledge and information can only lead us to the right door; it cannot make us walk through it.

Technology functions a lot like knowledge in this way. While I want to use it to bring about change, it rarely does in and of itself. I find new advances in technology to be interesting and engaging, but powerless to bring about a change of heart. I've bought more calendar programs than there are days of the year, simply because they promised to bring order and peace of mind to scheduling and ease to setting up and confirming appointments. But

I've learned the hard way that the best organizational tool on the market cannot override the issues of the person using the tool. Employing all the latest bells and whistles, alarms, alerts, and now music, the app that runs my calendar does a great job of reminding me about every date I have, but it cannot help me know when to stop adding new appointments or how to prioritize my schedule in the most meaningful way.

If knowledge alone can't make us change, and technology in all its glory is impotent to motivate us, then changing must be tough to do. If changing our patterns and our habits were as easy as changing clothes or the dirty sponge by the sink, we'd all be changing a lot more things about our lives and the way we live. Changing anything about ourselves takes work. I often shake my head over the simple solutions people offer to others. While "advice" falls under the information category, advice is different from information in that it is a solution offered to you personally, usually by someone you know.

If I had a nickel for every time someone suggested balance as a solution for crazy, I could buy my own beam. It is terrible advice, not only because I don't think balance is possible, but also because it's impossible to balance things that aren't equal. Now, if balance means steadiness or stability, more yoga, or just not falling down all the time, I'm good with trying to find more balance. But if balance means making life "balance out" as if it were a checking account—spending equal time working and not working, being with your kids as much or more as you're away from them—then this advice is a problem, not a solution.

If simple pieces of advice could bring about change, no one would ever wear torn underwear or go out in the rain without an umbrella or look a gift horse in the mouth. But life is much more complex and change is hard and giving others advice is useless. In fact, to bring about lasting change, I find advice the least effective agent of the three I've mentioned. When you can't make a forty-pound kettlebell and a Cheerio balance, you feel worse than you did before you got the advice! And now people are watching to see if you're taking their advice! Sigh. I have considered entering the Witness Protection Program to be free of all this. Work and family are not equal in the hearts of parents and never will be. Can we release this idea of finding balance in our lives? Can we quit offering balance so freely as the answer to crazy? Maybe if I was in control of every aspect of life, I could balance it out like a healthy meal on a compartmen-talized Hello Kitty plate, but my life is not always my own to control. When my child comes down with the stomach flu or my mother has a stroke, I don't think, *Hmm, how am I going to balance this?* I just make peace with limping. When financial realities call shotgun, the priorities get shuffled yet again. There are many times I have to work when I would rather be home or have to be home when I need to work. Balance, schmalance.

Wanting to create calm in my life was not enough to bring it about. None of the advice, technology, or information I sought for help could bring it about. But the emotional earthquake that split me in two would ultimately bring about the change. When some unseen fissure in our friendship became a crack and my friend decided to hit Send, it broke apart the joy of more than a decade of friendship and shifted the very foundation on which I stood. I would not know it for some time, but this crisis held as its hidden offering the power to create calm.

THE POWER OF A PERSPECTIVE-ALTERING EVENT

Author Kathleen Norris writes, "The word *crisis* derives from the Greek for 'a sifting' . . . to jostle, sift and sort things until only what was most vital would remain."[3] Recently, I accompanied my son's class on a field trip to sift for gold. Elliot and I put our pans into the bottom of the riverbed and scooped up sand and rock and began sifting, shaking, jostling the pans from side to side. Because the gold is the heaviest thing in the pan, it sinks to the bottom, and the sand and rock float away in the water as you continue shaking and sifting. If you're lucky, the gold is what remains. If there is no gold in your pan, you scoop and sift again, and again.

In the book of Job, God gives permission for Job to be "sifted"—and man oh man, was he ever. Yet through this horrific and wrenching sifting, God found gold in Job, and Job found the hand of God holding him through it all. We simply cannot sift our own hearts in the same way that a crisis can. I know I couldn't. I would be way too quick to make peace with the rocks and sand and give up on ever finding gold.

I'm not unfamiliar with the process of sifting. This was not the first crisis I had gone through, nor will it be my last. I wouldn't be a dramatist, or an author, or even a mother were it not for the perspective-altering events that sifted my life and my soul. As hard as going through each crisis was, the perspective that was created in its crucible was transformational gold.

I've written about two of these PAEs in previous books, and if you've read *Fresh Brewed Life*, you'll know that the perspective of finding hope in the daily grind came from processing the pain in my early life. I wrote a lot about the sifting that occurred in my heart following my parents' divorce when I was five—much of which I didn't and couldn't process until my midtwenties.

In *Keeping a Princess Heart in a Not So Fairytale World*, I wrote about my struggle to keep a soft heart in the midst of the hard world of pain and disappointment. Going through the sifting of my own divorce at thirty-four I recognized my tendency to gravitate toward extremes. Torn apart, I sought to resist phony idealism, but neither did I want to give in to harsh cynicism. I needed to forge a perspective between the two that could keep me out of either destructive extreme.

If you've gone through a perspective-altering event at any point in your life, you know exactly what I'm talking about. You may not call it a PAE, as that is a term I just made up, but whatever you call it—crisis, sifting, dark night of the soul—you know. You've had to face something you never wanted to face, such as:

- Cancer, in you or in someone you love
- Divorce, wanted or unwanted
- Death of a child or spouse or family member or close friend
- Disease or illness
- An accident

- An unwanted job change
- Major surgery
- Chronic pain
- Rejection or betrayal

These and numerous other crises pierce our lives and alter our perspective. We don't see things the same way after something like cancer interrupts; we can't. Life doesn't continue on as usual; it's different forever. Following a divorce or losing someone through death, we know life will go on, but we also know it will never be the same.

Over the years of sharing my experiences I've been privileged to hear the stories of many others as well. For all the different and personal details, the arc of the story is almost always the same: You're going along happily without appreciation of how good you have it, and then the phone rings, the papers come, the discovery is made, the truth becomes known, the police knock on your door . . . all of a sudden and without much, or any, prior warning, a big hole opens up in the earth around you and you drop down into a world you didn't know existed. Or if you knew it existed, you never paid any attention to it. Abruptly, you're in "funeral world" looking at caskets, thinking, *I do not want to be here*, and you notice there are six other families around you thinking the same thing. Other people, the kind you were just yesterday, aren't shopping for caskets; they're at Costco shopping for toilet paper. You hate them and wish you were them at the same time, but you can never go back.

I could never unread that email. Life would never be the same going forward.

Like one writer in the Psalms expressed, day and night tears were my food.[4] I couldn't stop crying, I couldn't eat, and I couldn't sleep. I couldn't return to life as normal because it simply wasn't normal anymore. Some different world was emerging through my tears and it looked blurry, dark, and confusing. This was Rejected by a Friend World and when blurry meets weary, days become bleary. I couldn't clear my vision or the emotional rain that just seemed to pour down hour by hour, day after day.

Life continued to go on around me, but I was not going on with it. My spirit would not rise up to lighten the burden; my heart could not pull itself back together. I had no idea what to do, so I did nothing.

STUCK IN A MOMENT

One thing I discovered during that time is that when the mind can't make sense of something important, it is very reluctant to let it go. It's almost as if your mind says, "Wait, don't move on; I need more information before I can go forward." It keeps returning to the trouble spot over and over, trying to figure it out. Like some weary detective stuck in the rain, my brain kept returning to the scene, retracing the steps, looking for clues, trying hard to solve the mystery of The Day Life Fell Apart. If I could have solved it, I could have moved on. But the mystery remained a mystery and more questions surfaced and my brain could not let it go. The detective became a stubborn donkey and sat down, refusing to move. I was stuck.

The band U2 won a Grammy for their song "Stuck in a Moment," which was about a friend's suicide. The song is a lament. It describes the friend's negative thoughts, the endless tears, and her inability to pull out of her sadness. She was stuck in a moment. I've heard others describe this inability to go on as being frozen in fear or paralyzed by anxiety, confirming my feeling that when the brain itself can't figure something out or make sense of it, it refuses to continue with business as usual—even if that business is life itself. I prayed, I sat still for long periods, I curled up in the fetal position, but as far as participating in my life, I might as well have been in the hospital. I can't count how many times I wished I was.

I fantasized about checking myself in. Not to a psych hospital, but to Room 202 at the general hospital. I would pretend I had some horrible, rare, contagious disease. I desperately wanted a break from people. I wanted a break from having to be okay. I wanted a break from the daily crazy of life while I tried to think and heal.

I needed a quiet place to be stuck without worrying about my kids' worrying about me. When they see me cry they get very sad and want to make it better. They want to know why I'm crying. I didn't want to tell them, but I didn't want to confuse them either. I feared if I didn't tell them something they would think they had done something wrong. I knew this all too well from my own childhood. I shared with them that Mommy had a hurt, like an owie, in my heart over a choice someone made. They seemed to understand, but I knew I needed to get it together, if only for them. I wanted time and a safe place to get unstuck, but there wasn't time or space to be found.

As a mother, I can't ever just call in stuck. No mother can—unless she happens to actually *be* stuck somewhere physically. Then someone else calls in on her behalf. "I'm sorry, Sally, Nicole won't be bringing the cookies today; she's stuck in the Sudan fighting human trafficking." Apart from that, how do you say, "Hello, would you mind coming over to watch the kids so I can just sob and work on my 'stuckness' for a few hours? I don't want to worry anyone, but I need to fall apart." Hmm, probably not going to happen, even though it should!

Sadly, at first it was easier to give up and give in to the dangerous kind of thinking that had made my life crazy in the first place. *Who can run this circus but me? You can't get stuck; you can't even go to the bathroom without the kids trying to kill each other! Pull it together Nicole and put a smile on it!*

Not only is this kind of thinking pointless, it is destructive and downright false. Because if I really was ill, or in a car accident, people would have to figure out how to get things done without me. We cannot be so afraid that things will fall apart that we fail to take care of ourselves when we know we need to. We must choose the road of vulnerability and call in stuck before someone else has to call on our behalf for reasons that aren't as funny as pretending to be in the Sudan. "Hello, this is Nurse Sally, and I'm calling from General Hospital about your wife."

Women don't pay attention to their symptoms. I don't. Not as much as I should, anyway. I never think I have the time. *So there's a little pain between my shoulder blades? Big deal! I still have two lunches to make, a check to write to the school, and four thousand errands to run this afternoon. Besides, whatever is going on between my shoulder blades that is making my arm feel hot is nothing compared to what's been going on in my right knee. When things slow down a bit, I've got to get that knee looked at or I won't be able to chaperone the field trip to the museum next week.*

It would be so interesting to be a fly on the wall watching two women simultaneously go about their days. In each household the woman is taking care of any number of tasks, mostly in response to, "Mom! I need . . . Hey, honey, I know you're busy, but could you . . . Mom, I need to be picked up after . . . Mom! You forgot to bring me . . . !" Then, with no warning, woman B falls to the floor. She is having a heart attack. This partly funny, mostly awful scene reveals more truth than we would like to admit or dare discuss. More women will die from heart attacks this year than from any other cause, including cancer![5] This is not a new thing. I looked up the stats for every year, going back fifteen years. Under age fifty, a woman's heart attack is *twice* as likely to cause death as a man's.[6] There are many factors that contribute to this, but one of the most significant is that women do not heed the early warning signs that would save their lives.

Fortunately, I didn't have a heart attack, but this fact only made it harder to answer the casual "How are you doing?" questions. I didn't know what to say. I didn't want to lie or hide my pain, but there didn't seem to be a succinct way to say that the earth had swallowed me whole. Strange, but if I'd had a heart attack, I would just say that. Instead, I answered, "I'm doing okay, thanks." And try to make it to my car before the tears started again. *You're not the first person to be rejected by a friend! Get over it!*

Mercifully, I didn't listen to that voice. I knew I couldn't get over it, not on my own anyway. I was in trouble. Despite the fear and the negative voices, I sounded the alarm. I told Roy and a couple of close friends, "I'm going down. I need help. Something has gone terribly wrong inside me."

My husband immediately stepped in to help with the routine of our lives. Other friends picked up the kids from school and even brought food. I watched through zombie-like eyes, grateful for their help, but uncertain as to what was happening and, more pressing, how I would find the strength to step back into life.

Because I couldn't move and because I couldn't do anything, I accidentally, or providentially, learned to be still in a deeper way than I had ever been able to. And the world didn't fall off its axis. I took the space I needed to grieve, privately. I took time to stare into the void, hoping for answers that might surface.

This was not calm yet; but it was stillness. I wasn't processing the awful in real time, but I was, albeit unknowingly, allowing crisis to be my teacher. Pain had focused my attention and pried open my soul with a crowbar. Pain had become a mouthpiece for God. Rather than run away from the pain or try to get out of it, I stayed very still and quiet; I was listening.

Long before the crisis hit, I'd wanted to create calm in my life and had attempted to bring it about, but it had not come. None of the information, technology, or advice I'd been given had been able to help me create calm in my life either. And then, right in the middle of the crazy, a crisis occurs, bringing a hidden power to change my perspective on life. Coincidence? Not a chance. Divine intervention.

If I could survive this crisis, I knew I would learn from it.

CHAPTER 3

Held

A COUPLE OF YEARS AGO, I was sitting outside on the front porch of our house, talking with a friend, when I heard the ice-cream truck coming. Abigail, who was five at the time, heard the truck as well. She came racing out the front door and bounded down the steps toward the street, passing me in a flash of pink. I hurried inside to find cash while she yelled for Jamal, our ice-cream-truck-driving friend. As I came out of the house, I could hear Abigail down the street a ways, still yelling as Jamal drove past her without stopping. I'm sure he never heard her or saw her, but Abigail was crushed. She started crying, which turned into sobbing. She had taken what happened so personally. I understood her disappointment and wanted to comfort her. "I'm so sorry, sweetie. I don't think Jamal even saw you, but it feels awful, I know." I tried to put my arms around her. With lightning speed her sadness turned to anger, almost rage, and she screamed, "Get him back, Mommy! Call him, call him!"

I tried to explain to Abigail that I couldn't call him. I did not have Jamal's cell number and I had no other idea of how to reach him. "We could drive around our neighborhood and look for Jamal," I offered. No dice. I suggested that he might come around the block again. At least that is what I hoped and prayed would happen. Abigail was inconsolable. The awful was descending upon her. She threw herself on the floor, rolling around, kicking and screaming like a wild animal. She was lashing out at anything and everything, including the one who loves her more than life itself. As soon as I could get close to her, I grabbed her and held on. She did not want to be held, but I would not let her go. My arms became the straitjacket to keep her safe in this intense time of pain.

It's possible you are thinking that Abigail is a spoiled little girl who throws a fit when she doesn't get what she wants. You might be right. But having given it thought, I don't think so. You see, in my desire to try to fix her pain

I offered to take her to get what she wanted. "Let's go get ice cream somewhere else," I suggested. "The exact kind you wanted from Jamal!" Again, nothing doing. No deal, because it wasn't about the ice cream. Abigail felt rejected by Jamal, her friend. She wanted him to come back and explain why he had passed her by. She was hurting like crazy. Apart from putting out a warrant for his arrest, I could not fix this one. There isn't enough ice cream in all the grocery stores in California to fix this kind of pain. Only Jamal could have helped in that moment, and he wasn't coming back.

This was an ache I could feel in my gut. I knew this pain too well.

THE QUESTION BENEATH THE QUESTION

This was the same pain I felt over the loss of my friend. She didn't pass me by in a truck, but she did pass me by, and everything inside me screamed as loudly as Abigail had. *Get her back here! Right now! Someone, anyone, call her, fix this, and get her back. Why did she keep driving? Doesn't she want to apologize? Doesn't she know how much this hurts me?*

But these questions were unanswerable. Pain has a way of squeezing questions out of us, but they are not always the most helpful questions at first. *Why did this happen to me? What was she thinking?* But if we keep letting our pain spill out, we'll eventually get to more helpful questions that can lead us closer to emotional health.

A number of years ago, a friend introduced me to a website called QBQ.[7] It means the Question behind the Question. The site is built around John G. Miller's book of the same title. It's a business book that calls for personal accountability in the workplace. Miller's aim is to help people in the workplace get to the heart of the issues without wasting time on surface questions like who is to blame. Miller suggests the question behind that question is the better one: What can I do to improve this situation?

My initial questions regarding this rupture in my friendship came fast and furiously. *What did I do? Why did this happen? What was she thinking? Was she even thinking?* While these questions are understandable and common and often the first ones we ask, I knew they weren't going to help me. Not only were these questions not going to be answered, I had the feeling they weren't the real questions anyway.

Because somewhere between stuckness and stillness, a new question—a really good one—came to mind: *When in your life have you felt these feelings before?*

That was the question that would lead me to search for an answer on my side of the breach. That was the QBQ, the Question behind the Question, or as I have referred to it since, the PBP, the Pain beneath the Pain.

THE PAIN BENEATH THE PAIN

One of my favorite theologians, Bruce Springsteen, said in a *Nightline Up Close* interview, "Everything you write about happened to you before you were twelve years old . . . You're always trying to sort that stuff out, and you never do."[8] So much of our adult pain, and certainly our most challenging relational pain, mirrors some kind of pain from childhood. My friend Amy says, "If it's hysterical, it's historical." But because the pain is creating a new, fresh wound, we don't recognize it as connected to old pain. This explains why we deal with the same core issues over and over. We have new eruptions of old wounds, but "The First Cut Is the Deepest."[9]

My pain was no exception, but I didn't think to look deeper until I asked myself, *When in your life have you felt these feelings before?* The image that surfaced in my mind was of a little girl sitting outside her mom's bedroom door, crying. I was seeing myself, and I was sobbing uncontrollably. I had done something that had hurt my mother and she was angry with me. She had gone into her bedroom, slammed the door, and locked me out. If history was to be repeated, I knew she wasn't going to come out for a long time.

RESISTANCE

The minute I felt that awful, too-familiar shame, it was like the sifting of my crisis revealed the emotional gold. There it was, a fresh cut on a very old wound. I'd like to tell you my first response was to begin to care for that wound, but my immediate response was to recoil and run. I had deep resistance to the very idea of moving any closer to it.

My brain and heart were on high alert. *Don't go any farther. We know what this is. This is pain—that's why it's way down here. We have felt this pain before and it's baaaad. It's dark and lonely in there, so just move along and fuggetaboutit!*

But I couldn't forget about it. I hadn't been able to move along. I was stuck in the awful. This rupture had brought up pain that was deeper and older than my friendship. There was childhood pain beneath my adult pain, and now both felt like they were killing me. *Haven't I already dealt with this old pain? Didn't I resolve these issues in years of therapy? Mom and I are fine!* And true to shame's form and tricks, I felt shame for feeling shame.

It's no wonder I found it easier to stay busy and run from thing to thing. Who signs up to sit in their darkest feelings, trying to process them, just waiting for despair to show up?

I feared that if I got too close to these feelings, the pain would be unbearable. If I started crying, I might never stop. What I really wanted was to stop feeling bad and to get back to normal; in other words, work. Productivity is a very seductive drug, and I was addicted. I couldn't be a bad girl if I was busy being a good one. Ugh. Sitting in the sadness of this great loss, unable to do much of anything, I began to have withdrawal from getting things done. Sitting still in the pain was the right thing to do, but still I felt a strong pull to clean the house, sweep off the back porch, rearrange the furniture, make some calls, vacuum out the lint in my coat pockets—whatever would distract, medicate, or numb my heart. *For goodness' sake, don't stop, get busy!* Like Dory, *Just keep swimming, just keep swimming!*

I remember days of just going through the motions, trying to do the next thing until it was bedtime. And no surprise to anyone but me, many of my crazy tendencies like multitasking and overcommitment had been serving a different purpose by distracting me from doing the most important work of all—facing my own fears of inadequacy and abandonment.

PERSISTENCE

I knew I had to keep pressing in toward that wound, despite the pain. Like some foolish Icarus heading toward the sun, what if I simply burned up on approach? Or melted away in pain and shame? Either way, I had to keep going to find out.

Anne Lamott writes in a recent blog post, "Crying is the way home: it bathes us, hydrates, moisturizes, waters the ground at our feet, where birds have been dropping seeds from the next house and country—so who knows what may grow?"[10]

I went back to the email that had brought my world crashing down months before and read the words again. Feelings of being bad washed over me, and confusion swirled around my brain again. Clearly I had done something terrible for this friend to pull away from me. Yet, rereading her words, I still had no idea what it was. Which left me with no idea how to make it right. Even if I had thought of something to do, there was no avenue in which to do it. The door was closed and locked. I had disappointed her somehow and not lived up to her expectations, even though they'd never been communicated to me. I had distressed her unknowingly, simply by being myself.

This was my mother all over again, and I never would have seen it or had the opportunity to deal with it had my friend not been trying to protect herself from something that was no threat: a good friend. What her response to me had exposed were the number of nerve endings that were still raw from childhood rejection. Of course they had been there all along, but when my friend went in her room and locked the door, leaving me sitting outside wondering what I had done, she unintentionally gave me a great gift: the path to the wound that was still hurting me. Finally, I could take care of it. I could clean it, bandage it, and help it get well.

My mom was just a young girl when she had me and I was the youngest of three. Mom did not know how to put words to her really big emotions. When she felt angry or hurt, she had to run away to create a feeling of safety and space for herself. Mom and I have discussed this many times over the last decade, beginning when I published *Fresh Brewed Life*.

While I know this now, I didn't process it this way as

a child. I couldn't. What her withdrawal created inside me were deep feelings of rejection and shame. I had no idea what I had done or why my mother had gone to her room and locked her door, but my mind, unable to understand her grown-up reasons, put forth to me that it must be my fault. I was bad and was the cause of all this drama. My little heart and mind experienced her silence as punishment and her withdrawal as rejection. I was bad, so bad that my own mother had to run away and lock the door.

HEALING

There is a reason the story of Abigail and Jamal made this book and opened this chapter. The pain of rejection runs deep in me. So deep, in fact, there are times I can't tell the difference between being rejected and just feeling the pain of old rejection. And while they can feel the same, they are not the same, and it is critical to know the difference. Abigail was not rejected. Jamal did not know how desperately she was calling for him. He never even heard her or saw her. It was not personal.

But because I was connecting the dots in my own story, I knew how to step in when Abigail felt rejected. I could help heal the pain that Abigail felt because of my own pain. My knowing was costly, but on that day, being able to give it to my daughter, it was priceless. I can't imagine the damage I would have caused by telling her, "Get over it. Life isn't always fair." We comfort others out of our own woundedness if we are lucky enough to know what it is.

HELD

I decided to share the Pain beneath the Pain with a friend who knows me well and who knew the rejection and rupture that had occurred. I carefully described the image that came to me when I'd asked myself, *When in your life have you felt these feelings before?* I described that little girl sitting outside her mother's bedroom door. Little girl tears spilled out and rolled down my almost fifty-year-old face. "What did I do, Mommy? Why are you mad at me? Please come out, I'm sorry." My head was down and I couldn't even make eye contact. I tasted the shame and pain of rejection in every salty tear.

I finished my story and my friend was still sitting right there, wiping tears as well. I was understood and received in my pain, but this comfort was much more than that. I was being held in the middle of the awful, in a way that felt as if I had gone back in time and the pain had just happened right then. There had been no one to comfort me. The person who could have held me was behind the locked door. I was alone in that memory, but I was not alone now. I was getting a do-over. The painful retelling had brought up the old shame and rejection, but the ending was different. This time I was being held as I cried. For a reason I don't think I'll ever be able to fully explain, this brought subterranean healing, deep and transformative. That old story, entrenched in my memory, had been unearthed as I told it, but it was changing. I never had to go back in time and be that little girl again. I would never have to live another day in that same pain. Dug out like an embedded rock of radioactive material, it began to shrink when exposed to the air and could now be disposed of properly. In this way, our friends hold divine power to receive us and even heal us from the tight grip of shame.

Our friends can see things in us and about our stories that we cannot. My friend could see in me what I could not see in myself. My mom's decision to withdraw to her room and lock the door did not mean I was bad or responsible in any way for her choice. I was overcome with compassion for that little girl inside me, but it took someone else to release her from the grip of shame. I never had to be that confused, crying little girl ever again.

As the compassion for that little girl inside me grew, I felt compassion anew for my mother. She had not intended to cause me such pain, but it had spilled out from her own unresolved pain. My mother had a difficult childhood, full of her own feelings of inadequacy and rejection. Healing was coming from that little girl inside me all the way up to the present as I felt love for my mother mingled with deep sadness for her pain and her lack of tools to manage it.

And in a moment I would never have expected, I felt a very similar compassion mingled with sadness for my friend who felt she had no choice but to close the door on me.

The core of pain was finally out after forty-five years.

In one of the Sundays that followed this catharsis, Noah Needleman, the worship leader at our church sang an original song, having no idea whatsoever that he'd written it for me. How could he know? We'd hardly met, but when he sang these words, "You formed me, you found me, and you held me, and you hold me still,"[11] I knew of what he sang in the deepest parts of me. Just as I'd held Abigail, I could feel that God was holding me. I'd stopped rolling around and crying as the strong arms of God wrapped around me to hold me and hold me still. But for this, I remain convinced I would have hurt others or hurt myself trying to get away from that confusing, awful pain of rejection. Mine had been the arms to hold and comfort my own heartbroken little girl as she felt rejected. I held her and I hold her now, mirroring the everlasting arms that continue to do the same for me.

I asked Abigail just this afternoon if she remembered Jamal passing her by that day, and surprisingly (and thankfully) she had no memory of it. As for me, I will never forget it. It was the day my arms were used to comfort my daughter with the very comfort I had longed for when I was a girl.

This deep sense of being held allowed me to feel safe and strong. My heart was coming back to life, and it was a calmer heart. A more assured heart. It was a heart that had survived the awful. And after all that watering from weeks of tears, I discovered what was growing next: a heart that was ready for a place of its own.

PART 2

Creating Calm on the Inside

CHAPTER 4

Room

I'M GOING TO HAVE a difficult time finding the right words to describe an encounter with someone I needed to get better acquainted with: myself. I would skip sharing it if it weren't such a critical part of my journey to calm. I'm chasing a mystery with words that are going to fall woefully short, but still I want to try, if only for someone else who needs this piece of the puzzle as much as I did. It was this piece that helped me visualize a safe place inside myself, a real home, a room of my own.

I'll try to set the scene to give context. It was a Friday evening session during a Seasons Weekend. Dr. Curt Thompson began by inviting all the attendees to get still and focus their attention in preparation for the weekend ahead. I wasn't going to participate in this exercise. After all, it wasn't really for me, it was for the attendees. I thought, *I'm not just an attendee, I'm the founder for crying out loud; I already know this stuff!*

I suspect that reading this will not be the same as being there, but I'll do my best to describe what happened. I've written Curt's words in bold (they are the important ones) and in the order he presented them. For your amusement, I've added my thoughts, more or less as I remember them, in italics beneath his words:

I'd like to invite you all to close your eyes for a few minutes.

Oh no, don't tell women to close their eyes on a Friday night after such a long day! They're going to fall asleep. I think I'm falling asleep! Curt, this is not *the way to start a life-changing weekend.*

Now focus your attention on your own breathing.

People are not going to want to pay attention to their own breath. Why didn't he pray first? What if people think this is a New Age practice? What if they think this is creepy? What if I think this is creepy? Nicole, just rest and think about your breathing! Your own *breathing.*

Allow yourself to feel the rhythm of your breath as you inhale and exhale slowly.

Okay, good, something specific. Yes, I can feel the rhythm of my inhale and exhale and I can smell in my breath the cof-fee I had before the session. C'mon, Curt, get to the intention part. Nicole, this is why you need the very weekend you've created.

You may find yourself distracted or your mind wandering . . .

Great, Curt can read my mind. Don't be silly! There isn't a man alive who can read a woman's mind. Do. Not. Laugh. Out. Loud.

If you do, just gently, and without judgment, return your thoughts to the rhythm of your breathing.

Good, inhale, exhale. Lead your distracted mind back to your coffee breath. Curt said without judgment, Nicole. Okay, that's good. I am judging myself right now for stinking at this exercise.

Now picture a place in your mind, somewhere you've been, perhaps somewhere you'd like to go, a place you've only seen in a picture—somewhere that feels peaceful and beautiful.

A spot came to mind immediately. It was a place I'd visited many years before on a very special trip. This spot still takes my breath away whenever I picture it. It's not that it was the most beautiful place I've ever been; it's not even that it was the most peaceful or serene place. It was the combination of all of that and more, tucked away from the main areas that were busy and crowded—and the first time I saw it, something stirred inside that made me feel something like what I hope heaven will feel like. Not hearing harps and sitting on clouds or even walking on streets of gold (we really don't know, do we?) but feeling the deepest sense of being safe, free, and, dare I say it, home. A very strange feeling washed over me that day; it was a yearning I hadn't felt in years. An aching, yearning for home.

At Curt's interruption, um, direction, I pictured myself walking around in my space. And in my mind, I sat down on a little bench in this lovelier than lovely spot. I felt the same peace I'd felt years before when I was there. I'm sure my hands had relaxed and my blood pressure had dropped and my breathing was steady and peaceful as I sat very still in my space, allowing this peace to penetrate my soul. I have no idea if it was two minutes or twenty-two minutes, but it was enough time for me to forget I was in an exercise, which is saying a lot. My inner commentary had ceased, which is incredibly noteworthy for me, and I was in this space, taking in the beauty and experiencing peace, fresh and new in that moment.

I've never felt anything quite like it before or since.

And somewhere off in the distance, I heard Curt

calling us to bring our attention back to our breathing and to the space where we were sitting. I was annoyed.

Wait! I'm not finished. I want to stay longer. I found my space! I'm in my space!

But I had to listen; after all Curt had helped me find this place, so I focused my attention once again on my breathing and I opened my eyes slowly, blinking and adjusting to the different light in the room. As weird as this may sound to you, and I understand if it does, I had a very deep sense that I had just gone somewhere very important. Part of my mind wanted to dismiss the experience immediately. *What was important about where you just went? What was that exercise anyway? People aren't going to understand. They'll just think it was some corny meditation . . .*

Before I could fall completely into cynicism, I noticed people around me wiping tears. Others in the room must also have had an encounter with a place that was meaningful to them. Perhaps they too had found a space for their souls, a safe, tucked-away niche they had not previously realized was available to visit any time they needed to get away. What was clear is that something had changed, and not just for me, although that was about all I could focus on as I wiped away my own tears.

PASCAL AND ME

I first encountered the writings of Blaise Pascal in college. I had no context or appreciation for a seventeenth-century French mathematician and philosopher. I was a bit more familiar with the writings of Edith Wharton, who stated knowingly, "Genius is of small use to a woman who doesn't know how to do her hair."[12] I read many of the greats during college to learn what I needed to know for the test. Years later I returned to Pascal's *Pensées* and discovered his incredible reflections about life and living. With the help of translators and the inimitable Peter Kreeft, I've come to value Pascal's timeless wisdom. In fact, many of Pascal's pensées, or thoughts, seem to apply better now than they did centuries ago when he penned them. Like this one: "I have often said that the sole cause of man's unhappiness is that he does not know how to stay quietly in his own room."[13]

Really, Blaise? (May I call you Blaise?) This is the *sole* cause of man's unhappiness? I can think of many more causes. And what about women? Oh right, we don't know how to stay quietly in *any* room, let alone our own room! I'm assuming that when Pascal wrote these words in the 1600s, he wasn't talking about being curled up in the fetal position in our rooms. I'm thinking he meant contentedly, peacefully at home with one's self. Could he have foreseen how difficult this would be for some of us? Especially for women? I'm guessing not, as it would still be three hundred years or so before the writer Virginia Woolf would assert, "A woman must have money and a room of her own if she is to write fiction."[14] This is true if a woman is to write anything, even a grocery list! Wolf's words came at a time when there were few women writers, mostly because women were not independently wealthy or free enough from responsibility to pick up a pen on their own, much less have a room all to themselves. While we've come a long way, baby, there is farther to go. Every woman (and man for that matter) should create a room of her own. Not necessarily a physical space, although that is significant and important, but an inner sanctuary, a sacred space, a room to sit quietly with one's real self. I agree with Pascal: our very happiness or contentedness with life depends on it.

I learned later that many Christian mystics created similar rooms. St. Theresa of Ávila called her space an "interior castle," while others described their places as secret gardens or even a citadel. These descriptions match my own experience of finding a place of strength and beauty. Each of the mystics, and probably each one of us, would describe our spot differently as this inner space is intensely personal, but many of the characteristics are the same: safe, strong, beautiful, holy, and full of light. But there is one characteristic that stands out to me more than the others used to describe this space: it almost always brings about an overwhelming sense of having come home.

COMING HOME

Home is a word unlike any other. The nuances of its definitions are complex because our very definition of *home* is dependent on our own experience. What feels like home to one person can feel like a prison to another. *Home* is a noun, as in our family home, and also an adjective, as in "this place feels home-y." But what does home really and ultimately mean? I confess, I haven't always known. It doesn't help that these days the concept of home is often reduced to chalk-drawn slogans in gift shops, like, "A house is made of walls and beams, but a home is built of love and dreams," or, "Home is where your cat is." Sweet, but not so helpful if you don't have a cat. So many sentiments and so little definition, especially for someone like me.

Growing up a child of early divorce, I found the feeling of home elusive at best. My father served in the navy, and before I was five we'd made at least that many moves. Over the next two years or so following my parents' divorce, both of them remarried, creating two separate and extremely different homes. Each family system had its own norms and traditions, which I often experienced as an outsider looking in. Traveling back and forth between homes several times a year, I never felt fully home in either one. I lived with my mother, who did her best to create a home wherever we lived, but it took a few more houses and two more husbands for her to get solid footing. I couldn't be happier to write that for the last thirty-five years with the steady love of a faithful husband, and a deep, trusting relationship with God, Mom has created a wonderful home and a sturdy life. While this settling has been a privilege to watch, it came much too late in life to help me while growing up. My developmental years were ravaged by strife, unrest, temporary and volatile relationships, and a deep sense of displacement, especially within myself. I rarely felt like I fit anywhere, and I'm not sure I ever did. As I traveled back and forth between homes, I felt that something was always missing and that I was always missing something. Life was never quite right, even when it was as right as it would ever be.

In my early thirties, the unthinkable became a

reality. I went through my own divorce. Having sworn to God and in front of everyone that what he had joined together no man or woman would put asunder, after thirteen years, asunder was all that was left. Years of counseling, undermined by compromises, untruths, and unresolved pain in both our lives, could not fix all that was broken. The undertow of inauthentic living had definitely pulled us under, along with any concept of home that we had shared. Adding my marriage to the pile of broken homes that had surrounded me was the greatest failure of my life. Until this point, those homes were in my past and none of the divorces were of my own choosing. But now my own marriage was over, and I was devastated inside and out; every home I'd known, including mine, wrecked. I held no illusions that I knew anything about home and harbored great fear that now I never would.

Previously, I have described what happened following my divorce as washing up on the island of misfit toys. It happened when my tired, wounded soul showed up to perform with the merry band of communicators involved with Women of Faith. The camaraderie, the shared calling, the sisterhood that is only possible in Christ, created the richest experience I'd ever had in community. I felt what it was like to really belong somewhere. Despite those personally awful years, I settled in to a place of welcoming love and deep friendship. This was not a taste of home; it was a full, sit-down meal.

By the fall of 2011, though, I was a new mother with two young children and well on the road to crazy. After a particularly difficult season, it became clear to me that it was time to step away from Women of Faith. Not from being a woman of faith, or from any of the friends and sisters I'd come to cherish, but from the organization and the travel. It was an extremely difficult decision as this had been my first real home and I'd been with this group for more than a decade. But even as it brought sadness, I felt clear about what I needed to do. I had to trust that the beauty of what this home had given me would not be lost if I stepped back. My hope was that this community and the love they gave me would be the very thing to support me in creating "home" for my own family.

Even with certainty about the decision, I felt that deep and familiar anxiety that once again I was leaving home. Part of me understood that this is what we do when we grow up. We leave home to create our own home and a home for others. And with a wonderful husband and two growing children, I would never have a better reason.

What I couldn't know at that time was that I'd never fully come home to myself. I didn't know what I didn't know. That discovery still lay ahead. The crisis I described in chapter 2 was about to hit and send me into the tailspin that would be the start of my long journey home.

There is nothing money can buy that is worth having if we can't come home to ourselves. There is nothing that will bring us more contentment at the end of a long day than getting home and being "at home" with your own soul. Equally, there is not much that can create more unhappiness and restlessness than never feeling at home when you get home or anywhere else. And that Friday night when Curt invited me to picture a real place of strength and beauty, I pulled back the curtain to reveal a room of my own. I discovered a personal and intimate space inside myself, a beautiful, inviting spot that would be with me wherever I went. I was home.

A ROOM OF MY VERY OWN

Part of me wishes I could have started telling this story right here, from home, from this peaceful place. I wish I could share truths with you that come out of decades spent quietly in my room, but I got here as quickly as

I could, and, I'm trusting, right on time. On time to encourage you to never give up searching for home. On time to let you know it's never too late to embrace a new way of living. On time to reassure you there is no need to fear a crisis because you cannot control when it will happen or what it will bring with it. You don't have to embrace it, only receive it, trusting the pain will be God's mouthpiece to speak love to your very soul.

As I spent time in my own room it became clear to me that I had been unable to hear what my crazy busy life was trying to tell me. I'd become deaf to my need for contemplation and rest. I'd suffered emotional hearing loss from the loud distractions constantly calling my name. Sheer busyness eroded my delight and joy, while praise for my talented multitasking deadened the feelings of despair I was trying to push down like trash in an overflowing can. Perhaps God knew it would take more than some friendly advice to break through the crazy, and so instead he used that awful pain like a giant megaphone to amplify his tender voice.

In Curt's wisdom, he helped us get back to our room or our spaces two more times over the course of the weekend. I'm sure he did this knowing how easy it would be for us to get lost on the way, or forget exactly where that pathway was. So twice more he walked us as far as he could take us and then left us to walk the last bit that only we knew. And sure enough, the way became more familiar each time. We are, after all, a bit like sheep. I have been known to go toward the wrong shepherd or wander off in search of food or some greener pasture. I'm thinking Curt also knew that the more times we heard the voice of Love calling us toward home, the more we would be able to recognize it and to come when we heard the call.

At fifty years old I am learning to sit quietly in my own room—a room that is everything that dark hallway was not. It's my home room. The place I return to again and again to hear God's voice of love and to spend time getting to know myself.

This room would serve as the space in which I would learn to appreciate the value of getting still, a treasure that couldn't be discovered from anywhere but inside my room.

CHAPTER 5

Still

ONE NIGHT, as I am saying goodnight to my son, I become increasingly frustrated by his inability to settle down and fall asleep. Elliot is in bed under the covers, teeth brushed, prayers said.

"Mom, I saw this amazing save by Jonathan Quick on YouTube! Let me show you what he did." And in a flash, Elliot is about to jump out of bed and do the splits like a goalie saving a puck in the Stanley Cup Finals.

I stop him quickly. "No, honey. First thing in the morning, okay? Right now it's time for bed."

"You know I'm really hoping to get goalie gear for my birthday."

"I know, sweetie. I'm going to turn out the light now."

My son has a gift for words, and communication comes naturally to him. He's very expressive for a boy his age. Like other boys, he's infinitely curious, but his curiosity and questions have words that shape his opinions and form persuasive arguments.

"I think it's safer for me to play with my own gear. You want me to be safe, right?"

"Absolutely, Elliot. That's why I need you to go to sleep right now."

"Okay, Mom."

"Thanks, buddy. I'm going to turn out the light now."

"Can we look for goalie gloves tomorrow after school?"

"Maybe, son, I'm not sure about my day tomorrow." At this point in the evening I'm not sure about my name, let alone tomorrow afternoon.

His brain gets going and doesn't stop just because it is bedtime. I ask him to lay still and quiet, but I might as well be asking him to build a 747 out of toothpicks! When he first tries to get still, *more* questions come out.

"Do you know how to calculate the circumference of a circle, Mom?"

"In *Clash of Clans* (his favorite iPad game at the moment) the level-four giants are the best. Can I tell you why?"

"Shhh . . . quiet and still, please."

"How come Frank in my class uses a lot of bad words?"

Frank uses bad words?! He almost had me.

"Buddy, right now it's time for sleeping, not more questions."

"But I don't know how to fall asleep!" he bemoans. Elliot has said this since he was four years old.

And I have said this since he was four years old. "You must stop talking now, son. Just lie here quietly, be still, and you will fall asleep!"

Then I lay down next to him and put my arm around his squirmy body. After five more questions and three more observations and an act of Congress, he finally gets quiet and then still. And I'm not kidding, in less than thirty seconds, he's *out*.

Falling asleep is never difficult; getting still and quiet is the real challenge.

When I say to Elliot, "Still and quiet, please," what I mean is, "Hold your body still (try to stop drumming, moving, tapping, fidgeting) and then quiet your mind, but first, your voice." But this is not easy. Far from it. It's hard, and not just for children. I know plenty of grown-ups who don't like to be still and quiet. I was one of them.

Roughly twenty-five years ago, I participated in a silent retreat with Brennan Manning. It was the opportunity of a lifetime, and I was grateful to get to do it, but it almost killed me! I'm not kidding. I felt lost and ineffective for five hours, uncertain of what I was supposed to be doing, which was nothing. Throughout my schooling, I maintained a 4.0 for talking, so not using one of my strongest gifts seemed wrong. I felt panicked and anxious over what others must be doing with this time. Surely it would be better than what I was doing with it! When the retreat was finally over, I was joyfully relieved to get back to talking. I remember talking nonstop to anyone who would listen to me about why extroverts should never participate in silent retreats!

It has taken me decades to get to this realization: I have spent more of my time trying to control the crazy on the outside than I have working toward creating calm on the inside. This was as big a revelation as the one that came in my late twenties when I finally understood that the way you look on the outside matters, but only a fraction as much as who you are on the inside. In the same kind of shift that turned my attention in my twenties from the external to the internal, my attention has turned once again to the inside to provide the way to creating calm.

˙GETTING STILL IS HARD

I've never talked to anyone who thought that getting still was a bad idea or practice. But most people must think it is a good idea for someone else, because only a handful of people set aside the time to do it. Why?

Silence Is Uncomfortable

Silence creates some level of anxiety in all of us. Consider the mild discomfort that happens in a program or even church service when, without explanation, everything gets really quiet. People assume something has gone wrong and begin looking around or shuffling papers. Think of the major discomfort created by "the silent treatment." Because a healthy relationship is marked by plentiful communication, the withdrawal of words creates a void that is uncomfortable and confusing at best, punishing at worst. And the granddaddy of all silence, solitary confinement, creates deep, deep discomfort and trauma. Our minds do not do well in the punishing silence of isolation. Because we were made for connection and communication, solitary confinement is a horrible practice and the very definition of torture.

We are used to a high level of noise. Our world is noisy—cars, buses, airplanes, televisions, horns honking, sirens. Silence is the anomaly. Noise makes us comfortable in many ways. We've become so accustomed to it that some people can't sleep without white noise, the low-level hum of some kind of sound. Others can't work without background noise like the television or music. Because I am one of those people, I like to write in coffee shops or busy places so my mind has to tune out all the noise. Oddly, the noise helps me focus. For years I dreamt of writing in a quiet cabin somewhere in the mountains, but when I tried it, several times actually, it never produced what I thought or hoped it would. The extreme silence actually made it harder for me to concentrate.

Our brains know the familiar noises around us, taking in sounds we are not conscious of. Thus, when silence "happens," the brain immediately fears that something is wrong and needs to be corrected. It can be irritating when the kids are playing and making noise, but when everything falls silent, that is terrifying. *What just happened?* Without retraining our brains to trust intentional silence as good, our brains will continue to avoid the discomfort silence creates and seek distractions from it.

Distraction Is a Way of Life

Nicholas Carr, author of *The Shallows*, said, "Finding moments to engage in contemplative thinking has always been a challenge, since we're distractible, but now that we're carrying these powerful media devices around with us all day long, those opportunities become even less frequent, for the simple reason that we have this ability to distract ourselves constantly."[15]

It is plausible that the television ushered in the casual and impersonal disconnect. If people were watching a show that was boring or made them feel uncomfortable, they could change the channel and move on or avoid a subject altogether. This has affected everything from our conversation to our level of concentration. Now we have hundreds of channels, and we "flip around" indiscriminately, not only on the television, but also on our devices and in our conversations. "Hang on one second, I'd better get that!" Which means, *Don't take it personally when I turn away from you.* Instead of staying connected for any length of time, we connect and disconnect constantly. We have technological permission to give in to any and all distractions. When even short exchanges are interrupted, important things like long conversations, being still, and focused time for contemplation have become casualties of distraction.

It's not just technology that distracts us from thinking deeply or feeling pain; our distractions come in all kinds of shapes and sizes. Sometimes we call them "retail therapy" or "comfort eating" or even "binge watching." Distractions like these keep us from facing our difficult issues—issues that cannot be solved by shopping or eating or watching. We can check out, lying on the couch, binge watching *Game of Thrones* for hours, but eventually we have to check back in. Often, the life we check back into has become more difficult while we've been "away"—and we can't wait to check out again. Consciously and unconsciously, distractions prevent us from pushing pause on our lives for even twenty minutes. Twenty minutes spent in stillness would reap more benefits than retail therapy ever could, and would cost much less.

We care for our souls well when we consider the issues we may be avoiding and the purpose our distractions may be serving. Without recognizing when we are using the plethora of distractions available to us to avoid facing important issues, or having hard conversations or any conversations, we have stopped working to make the most of our lives and settled for working to escape from them.

If we can deal with our distractions, not eliminate them but illuminate them for what they are, we will be stronger for it. We will need all the strength that we can get as we face another obstacle on our way to stillness.

Fear Is an Aggressive Bully

I should have taken a class in college on how to face my fears, but I never saw it offered on any course list. If you wish you'd done this as well, as you have some fears of your own to face, try to sit quietly in your room and you'll find yourself in a graduate-level class!

Just thinking about facing our fears can make us feel afraid. Never forget: fear is a bully—an insecure, mean kid that feels better when you feel small.

One of the ways I stand up to the bully is to write my fears down on paper. Written down, fears often look silly. But regardless of whether or not they are legit, whenever I give in to fear, it grows. When I stand up to it for being the bully it is, fear diminishes and my strength increases.

Here are a few of the (yes, ridiculous) fears that make getting still difficult for me.

I fear I'll stink at this. In fairness, this fear has relatively little to do with the act of getting still. It's just another place this very personal fear shows up. I carry it with me like a watermelon to a picnic, so it would make sense how often it shows up when I'm heading to my room. *I don't think you're doing this "still thing" very well. Remember that silent retreat, Nicole? This isn't your* *strength. And what if you're doing this wrong? I bet Richard Rohr doesn't have this fear. Why don't you focus on your gifts and leave this stillness to those who have been doing it longer and can do it better?* When there is nothing to keep me from going down the rabbit hole of my own inadequacy, I have two choices:

1. Recognize the voice of fear and stand up to it to cross the threshold into stillness.
2. Listen to fear, believe it to be stronger, and go start cleaning out the garage.

I am empowered to stand my ground when I recognize that my fear is trying to protect something. If I go straight toward the fear with questions it must answer, I turn the tables and demonstrate that I am in charge. *Why are you so afraid of not being good at this? What would that mean? What if the whole world decided you were no good at this? What if Richard Rohr publicly said, "Nicole Johnson is no good at this whole stillness thing"? What would happen?*

Now I've gotten to the heart of my fear. Having identified this fear by name, it becomes much easier to tame. I take a minute to feel it, really think about it, and then walk right past it. Because I can say to that fear, "It doesn't matter to me if the whole world, including the fabulous RR, thinks I stink at this!" One of the reasons to move toward stillness is to uproot our fears of not being good enough—so it is working! Besides, how can I stink at something that is working so well? And who cares if I do? So there, fear!

I fear I'll get bored. Despite how many significant and meaningful times I've spent being still, something in me fears it each time anew. My mind whispers, *You are going to get bored.* I'm not sure where this fear of boredom comes from or if there was a time in my life when it really *began*; it seems to me that it is just part of the human condition, mine anyway.

My children fear boredom like some incurable disease they might catch. They panic and think I should be saving them from it like I would be if they were drowning in front of my eyes. It's hard to fault them too much as I know plenty of adults who also fear boredom. Some of my friends tell me they would prefer an insane life of busyness to being bored. Racing from thing to thing, living in constant stimulation, they offer, "Well, at least I'm not bored." I can't count the number of times I've been waiting in line behind a full-on grown-up who has been made to wait, and you would think having to stand there for a few minutes was going to cause a rupture in their aorta!

I am learning to face this fear by asking myself, *So what if you're bored? You haven't been bored before, but if you get bored this time, what is the big fat deal? What is the worst thing that can happen?* I have to remind my brain that fear is not in control. There is a new sheriff in town and boredom is not a bad guy!

I've actually found great freedom in boredom—not that I experience it much. But when I have, it was surprisingly pleasant, *Wow this is cool; I'm bored!* The fear of boredom is not rare or cool, but boredom itself is quite nice. I've come to see it as an indication that I'm getting still. And not surprising is how often creative thoughts or insights with divine fingerprints come straight out of the lovely boredom I feared so much.

I fear I'll feel worse than I already do. As an adult, I've never gone out of my way to spend time with myself until recently. (This doesn't mean I wasn't ever by myself; it means I never sought time alone with myself, on purpose, unlike accidentally getting stuck in an elevator, but that's a story for another time.) Until the moment I shared in chapter 3 of "being found," shame kept me afraid (subconsciously) that if I ever went back to that dark hallway, no one would ever come to find me.

This was a piece of the offering hidden in the crisis. The rejection by my friend sent me straight to that hallway, and I played my part just as I always had. The sad, alone, confused little girl who felt very ashamed by what she had done (whatever it had been). Dr. Curt Thompson writes in *Anatomy of the Soul* that when we are in "the grip of shame, we have a keen sense of painful isolation. We feel separated, not only from others, but disconnected within ourselves."[16] Shame will keep us in that state of confusion about our own feelings and separated from others. We have to choose the very connection, especially within ourselves, that feels terrifying in the moment. This is the way out of shame. It is the way to freedom.

I've already shared how healing found my little girl soul, but healing continues in the corridors of my mind every time I face this fear, which is almost every time I get still. I fear when I reflect over things I've neglected or when I acknowledge things I've done wrong, that shame is going to eat me alive. I'm not going to feel the "appropriate guilt" (I've done something wrong and can make amends); instead I am going to be consumed by shame, which feels like I'm just bad and I'll never be able to make things right.

To face this fear and continue to stillness, I simply have to point past it to that room that lies ahead. My own place of strength and beauty is the proof that I'm no longer that little girl. I have a room of my own waiting for me just up ahead. The light is on and the deep love of God is calling me. That is all the invitation I need to bid adieu to that "you're going to feel bad" fear and ask it to kindly step aside, for I have somewhere to be right now, and goodness is waiting for me.

I don't intend to communicate that I no longer have to face these fears. Nor do I intend to portray them as easy to conquer. They are menacing fears, not unlike big hulking guards, that show up most often at the passageway to stillness, trying to block my access. They want to make me afraid to go into my room. But knowing they are the self-appointed bodyguards of my mind trying to protect itself (from things it doesn't need to fear) makes it easier to fight them. Since I've named them and stood up to them, they seem to respect me. Sometimes they even let me pass without a fight, but they've also been known to be semi-polite and then try to trip me on the way in. Some days a new fear will show up, but being a little more familiar with the tricks and schemes, I find I'm more creative with ways to sidestep them and continue on my way to still and quiet. Because despite the struggle, once I arrive, the value of being still is worth far more than the challenge of all difficulties put together.

BEING STILL IS PRICELESS

We call something priceless when it cannot be replaced. We call something priceless when its worth exceeds the value of money, because money cannot provide it. Stillness (the process of sitting quietly in my own room) has brought things into my life that could not have come in through any other door. These are things I possess, but they are not "possessions." They could never be purchased and their value in my life is irreplaceable.

Here are three of them:

1. A deeper knowledge of self
2. A deeper knowledge of God
3. A created center of calm

A Deeper Knowledge of Myself

Richard Rohr writes, "Many people have never actually met themselves."[17] I think this is true for many reasons, but I don't think we know how to meet ourselves; I certainly didn't. I had no idea it took being still to become acquainted with myself. I wasn't spending a lot of time alone, not only because it felt uncomfortable and because I feared it; it just never occurred to me that it would be helpful for my sense of well-being. But how could I ever come to know myself and learn to enjoy my own company without spending time with myself?

For me, getting still has given me the unique chance to become better friends with my real self. It has taken time to coax her out of hiding and get to know her better. She is very funny, but often shy. She is smart, creative, and very nerdy. She enjoys solitude (who knew?) and loves to laugh even if no one else is laughing with her. She is becoming more confident as she emerges out of the shadow of the other self.

You see, I have another self too: my imposter self. She's the one that I dress up and send out into the world every day. She is the one who tries too hard to be perfect. She is the one who worries too much about OPO (other people's opinions). She is the one who will try to please over trying to connect. She will scold my real self if she's laughing too loud. She is polite in public, but not so nice in private. She is my imposter. My room is the only place my real self and my imposter self can talk to each other. Obviously they are both me, but only in the safest place of home can I do the hard work of bringing them into one. Stillness revealed the need for even deeper "integration" to be the most authentic me I can be.

As I got to know myself in the stillness, I found I was

encountering God differently. Stillness was facilitating deeper knowledge and a richer experience of God.

A Deeper Knowledge of God

"Be still, and know that I am God" (Ps. 46:10). The psalmist here is quoting God. Not that this is a commandment; after all it didn't make the top ten, but I would say this is a strong suggestion and *muy importante*.

My personal translation of this verse is: "I can be still and *know* that God is God, or I can stay busy and keep wondering if I am!" If I'm reading this psalm right, the path to knowing there is a God is being still enough to find out. Because when I am running my world, making all the decisions and calling all the shots, I am at the center of my own universe. When I play God so often, I forget I'm not God. I might even be serving God, but it is mostly in an advisory capacity.

There is an old joke worth sharing: "What is the difference between you and God?"

"I don't know, what is the difference?"

"God never gets confused and thinks he's you!"

Stillness provides me the opportunity to keep the "who is whom?" question answered correctly. It allows me to remove myself from the center of my own world, *again*. I confess to taking up a role I cannot play. I humbly bow before the greatness of God. These deep reminders always make me weep with relief and gratitude. I do want to be like God, but I do not want to be God. I know too well that trying to be God, even subconsciously, creates crazy inside and out.

Peter Kreeft's commentary on Pascal says as much: "We want to complexify our lives. We don't have to, we want to. We want to be harried and hassled and busy. Unconsciously, we want the very things we complain about. For if we had leisure, we would look at ourselves and listen to our hearts and see the great gaping hole in our hearts and be terrified, because that hole is so big that nothing but God can fill it."[18]

When I am busy playing God, I ignore God. I don't ask any questions of God or about God. I don't need to. I dig the hole a lot deeper and refuse to let him fill it. Or if I do ask a question, it's not a real question, and I'm not listening for an answer. When I'm doing the headless chicken thing I do, I bark questions that are not questions at all, such as, "Elliot, will you put your shoes on, please?" I'm not asking him a question; I'm making a request couched in a question. I don't listen for his response because I'm not expecting one! I'm expecting his cooperation with my directive. If he doesn't put his shoes on, I huff, "You're not listening to me, son!" When the truth is

I'm not listening to him. This is why extremely capable, busy, modern people dismiss the concept of God. They never stop to listen. They might ask hard questions of God, but God is rarely, if ever, given the chance to answer. *Why did my father die when I was nine? Why does the world have to suffer so horribly? Isn't it wrong that children are starving?* While these look like questions, they are not if people don't listen for an answer. They are merely rhetorical questions they think they know the answer to: Either God is not there or God does not care about me or the world. Instead of making assumptions about God, it would be more accurate to note that we are not listening or giving God an opportunity to speak to our questions. In order to do that, we would have to stop and be still and face the great gaping hole.

We can come to know more about God than we have ever dared to believe if we gave God the opportunity to respond to us. This would deepen our knowledge and our faith, but to do this we must be still. I can see this dynamic played out in my relationship with my kids. When I ask Abigail or Elliot to be still, they react as if I've asked them to scale the Great Wall of China using a plunger! But unless they can be still, especially when they need or want something, I cannot help very effectively. If Abigail is waving her glass in the air, I cannot fill it with water. *Hold it still, please.* If Elliot is hopping around, I cannot put a Band-Aid on his scraped knee. *I know it hurts, sweetie, but hold it still for just a second.* If I didn't see her fall and Abigail cannot stop crying to tell me what hurts, I feel helpless to make it better. *Take a deep breath, honey, take a minute and then tell me where it hurts.* I'm not asking the kids to be still for the rest of their lives, or mine, just long enough to allow me to pour the water, or care for the wound, or figure out how to help. Their stillness gives me the best chance to reveal my heart to them.

Isn't the implication the same for me with God? If I can't be still either, I am left longing, or wounded, angry, or worse, stuck in doubt that God exists. If I can't be still, I miss out on the very ways God wants to demonstrate his own character to me.

"Be still and know" is simultaneously a challenge, an invitation, a promise, and even a dare.

Not only has getting still deepened my knowledge of myself and of God, it has created a center of calm in my life.

A Center of Calm

The verses in Psalm 23 are some of the most comforting, calming words in all of Scripture: "He leads me beside quiet waters, he refreshes my soul." When I am troubled or trying to process something difficult, I can't imagine anything more helpful than a friend inviting me for a walk alongside a river or stream. This embodied image of God as a loving, caring friend who leads me on long walks beside still waters calms and restores my soul. So much so that I have incorporated the image into my place of strength and beauty.

Through getting still I have come to know calm. Calm is the promised land that lies on the other side of still. I couldn't have entered into calm through any other door than by being still. Crossing the awkward, fearful, sometimes emotionally treacherous terrain of still is what it took to recalibrate my mind and spirit to calm. It was a crisis that brought my workaholism to a stop and brought on withdrawal symptoms. The emotional work of stillness began to counter my unhealthy dependence on work as I sat by myself in seemingly unproductive quiet. In this way, still is a paradox; it isn't still at all. Water can be still without being stagnant as long as it holds life. Calm can be full of energy when it is harnessed by self-control. A calm life is not motionless or immobile; it is a life with great capacity and full of movement, but its pace is different and its motive is pure. In the way of paradox, it turns out that the peace calm has brought to my life has not slowed my productivity but increased it. I am accomplishing greater things when not driven by performance or fear of what others may think.

I know that it is difficult and seemingly impossible to set aside time to be alone and quiet. And yet, I hope I've made the case that the reward for doing so will bring more benefit than the skipping of it ever will. I can't overstate the help, the health, the calm, the value stillness has brought to my life. For me, there has been no substitute, then or now, that can produce the same result in my life. Learning to be still and quiet inside my own soul has created what I had only dreamed of: a center of calm.

CHAPTER 6

Homework

IT'S RISKY TO TITLE a chapter "Homework." It brings up bad memories of a boring teacher intoning, "Okay, class, [insert dry swallowing sound] here is your homework assignment for today." There aren't many words strung together in a sentence that can produce more eye rolling, groans, or general disgust. Not in my house anyway. (My husband might argue, "Honey, does my hair look okay?" comes pretty close, but I think terror is different from groaning, so it doesn't really count.)

In fairness to kids, homework really should be called schoolwork you have to do at home, not homework. About as inviting as sitting down to a bowl of melted ice cream, schoolwork that has to be done at home is a hard sell for most kids.

Despite the negative connotations of the word *homework*, I really need to use it here. It is the right word to describe a certain kind of work that can only be done at home, in your room. This is not housework, far from it. It is rest work. It's still-work. How can I say this best? It's not really work I do but more work that I submit to, work that I allow to be done in me when I am still and quiet. This is the very work that cultivates calm.

But I'm getting a little ahead of myself. I first need to explain the process that helps me get still so that I can do the homework!

DOWNSHIFTING IN ORDER TO TRANSITION

Sometimes I can take a few minutes in the early morning to get still and quiet, before the world wakes up. But more often, when I'm trying to get still my day has already shifted into gear and I need to downshift to transition into stillness. If I just stop in my tracks in the middle of all that I'm doing or thinking about or handling, I would run into myself about eight times! I have to downshift before I can get to a full stop. Whether I'm home or at work or even home at work, here are some of the specific things I do to downshift into stillness.

Use an Instrument of Time

Lately, I have been helped in transitioning from busy to still by using—don't laugh—a snow globe. Yes, I just wrote the words *snow globe*. Everybody has one from a gift shop from some place in the world. Go look for your globe; it is next to the fruitcake. This instrument of time functions like a clutch to help me downshift more smoothly.

My snow globe happens to be of the Harry Potter variety. I keep vowing to get a newer, cooler, more grown-up snow globe (which I'm thinking I should have done before writing this chapter), but fortunately the coolness factor of a snow globe has no effect on the practice itself. Any variety will do. So pick up your globe—or preferred instrument of time, be it an hourglass, the timer on your phone (slightly risky), a giant glitter ball, or a clock on the wall—and bring it with you to find your calm chair.

Find Your Calm Chair

You probably already know the one. It might be the ugly one, but pay no attention to its appearance, because its virtue is its comfort. If you took a poll of strangers, this chair is the one that would unanimously be named the most comfortable in the house. If your chair is sitting in the freeway of your house, go ahead and move it (or have someone else move it) to where you can sit away from the chaos. If you're able to get some quiet time at your office or at work, your chair can be there, especially if you have a door that you can close for some privacy. Your calm chair can even be your desk chair if you choose.

My calm chair is in my home office, but I had to move it there from the family room. It is the ugly chair, so no one was unhappy that it went down the hall. It is my calm chair because it's where I go when I want to get still. It envelops me, making it easy to stay there for a good while. Often just seeing my chair in the middle of the day and knowing it is right there waiting for me can bring a sense of well-being to my soul.

Always try to wear comfortable clothes when you sit in your calm chair. Your feet should be able to touch the floor easily and your back should be well supported. If you sit down and want to fall asleep, you've found your calm chair. Name it and claim it.

Focus on Breathing

While sitting in my calm chair, I shake up the globe and watch the snow swirl around furiously. While I'm waiting for it to settle, I begin to focus on my breathing. While inhaling and exhaling slowly, I observe gravity working inside the little world of glass. It's very peaceful, and sitting there taking deep breaths I can feel myself shifting into a lower gear and then into an even lower gear, getting prepared to stop.

Focusing on my breathing is a new thing for me. I can't say that I've ever paid this much attention to my breath until now. I'd never consciously been aware of how great it felt to take a really deep breath and then another one and then another one. Only in acting class had I ever practiced exhaling slowly and fully in order to support my breathing, and that was back in the day of pay phones.

Unless I'm focused on projecting for an outdoor performance or speaking publicly when I'm in danger of losing my voice, I hardly ever think about my breathing. Most of the time it is my posture or my level of activity that determines the depth of my breathing. Rarely (never) am I concentrating on sending oxygen to my brain. (Ah, it is all beginning to make sense now . . .) So when I focus on my breathing it's like I'm switching from defense to offense or from auto-pilot to manual controls.

I close my eyes and breathe in stillness and exhale

busyness. I picture my path and I breathe in the pure, clean air as I walk alongside still waters. I let go and breathe out the toxicities of worry and stress. After five or six deep inhales and exhales, I'll open my eyes enough to peek at the globe. I'm usually ready about the time the very last flake settles on Hogwarts.

I close my eyes again to visualize that beautiful space created inside my soul during that life-changing exercise at Seasons. Just as I left it last, it is still there, waiting for my return. I walk into this sacred place inside my soul, my home.

When I transition like this—in a comfortable setting I've prepared, focusing on calming breathing, and taking time to remember and "enter" my beautiful place, I am far more able to enter into stillness than when I don't. Transitions are a good friend to calm. They can make or break the event coming up, and they get me ready to do the kind of soul work that creates calm.

HOMEWORK = SOUL WORK

There is a way of contemplation, resting, and thinking that can only be done from the safest place imaginable: home. Not that I can't contemplate, think, or rest anywhere I go, because I can, and I do, but there is something very different about the way I think when I am sitting quietly in my room, in the space that is my inner home.

There is something deeper about the way I contemplate truth when I feel the security of love wrapped around me. The work that happens in the quietness of our rooms is not about our labor or toiling or striving; it is about surrendering and relinquishing control, and that is work of a different kind. I want to repeat this phrase: this is a kind of work that is best done from home.

There is enormous value in just sitting in your calm chair and getting to your mental place of strength and beauty and then sitting still. Period. You don't have to do anything and you will still reap nice rewards from doing all the work it took for you to get there. So don't stress about what you have to do during your time of stillness or how long it should be or whether or not you've been successful. Don't give in to any pressure to "make the most of it." Intentionally slowing down and getting to a place of stillness is already good work to be praised.

You may decide you want to set a goal of being in your room for a certain length of time or getting better at meditation or prayer. While these are worthy endeavors, do not allow anything to put pressure on your time of quiet or it will begin to lose the very value it brings. I have made the mistake of trying to "use" my time for accomplishing something (even good things like studying the Bible) only to find myself under pressure again.

For this reason, I rarely, if ever, have an agenda for what I'm going to do when I get to my room, mostly because I'm not going to "do"; I'm going to "be." And if I'm tired or sleepy, "being" often includes resting, which is holy work.

RESTING

I remember the excitement I felt the first time I went to my space following the weekend at Seasons. I was in my living room (before I had a study) and sat down in my calm chair, barely able to contain my anticipation of getting still and quiet. I was walking into my room in my mind's eye and taking in the beauty of the space. I felt overwhelmed with gratitude for my hard journey and what I could feel it was bringing about inside me. I was so still and I remember thinking, *Okay, now what?* Really. That's exactly what I thought. *It has taken me fifty years to get here. What should I do first? Nothing? How does one do nothing? If I am successful at this can I check off "nothing" from my list? Hurray! I finished doing nothing! I got nothing done and I'm so happy for myself.*

This still cracks me up. After everything it took to get me to this place—the crazy, the crisis, the deeper pain—the thought of instantly turning around and saying, "Well, that was nice. I'm not sure what to do here, so I'll be going now, goodbye," was too funny.

I was able to sit in my beautiful space with gratitude and tears. I spent time thanking God for the way he holds me and holds me still. I sank deeper into my calm chair and within ten minutes I was sound asleep. I kid you not. It might have been less than ten minutes. I woke up a little disappointed, but still so grateful.

Earlier in my life I might have beat myself up about this. But that day I could just smile at the comfort and ease I felt being home in the presence of God. I had just received something my body needed by putting myself in a place of care.

I'm reminded of a story I heard years ago about "falling asleep on God."

A man was asking his spiritual director how he would ever get better at prayer if he kept falling asleep trying to pray. The man felt like he wasn't effective in spending time with God because he kept drifting off every time he closed his eyes. The wise director asked his student, "How do you feel about your relationship with God when you wake up?" The man confessed he feared God's disappointment in him.

"What if you perceived God as an old man sitting

quietly in his rocker by the fire? God is reading or thinking and you are his dog, lying at his feet? Would that
change how you might feel when you wake up?"

It certainly did for me. A change in perspective is
no small change. I spent years viewing a relationship
with God as yet another thing I was responsible for
and therefore capable of messing up. I lived under the
weight of what I thought to be God's expectations, only
to discover they were my projections about God's expectations, and not the real thing. I do not believe God is
disappointed in me in the least when I fall asleep in his
presence, which I often do. It's possible his disappointment comes when I'm awake! I'm joking of course—I
don't believe God is ever disappointed in us.

So I include sleeping in God's presence as part of
homework or, more accurately, homesleep. This kind of
contented rest comes from a deep sense of peace and
comfort. When I see myself as that relaxed dog asleep at
the feet of her loving master, I rest with abandon. I rest
as one who is safe at home. This is the work of rest.

REFLECTING

I keep my journal, my Bible, and a few books that are
devotional in nature near my calm chair, and I might

reach for one of those to provide direction to get started. One book that I reach for often is a collection of Puritan prayers called *The Valley of Vision*.[19] I also have a book or two that offer short thoughts or guided meditations that will focus my attention on one particular idea worthy of contemplation. But apart from reading a brief passage or prayer, my time is spent in reflection.

Reflecting on God

I often use a tool called the Prayer of Examen by St. Ignatius of Loyola to help me reflect on God. I came to know this prayer only recently, but people have been using it as a meditation for over four hundred years. I guess it's the new "old" thing. This prayer has been more popular in other faith traditions than in the one in which I was raised, so I came to love it much later in life, but it has become a staple of my homework.

Examen is the Latin word for examination, and the prayer leads the participant through steps, beginning with becoming aware of the presence of God, followed by reviewing your day with gratitude. Fr. Dennis Hamm, a Jesuit priest and professor of Scripture at Creighton University, calls the Prayer of Examen "rummaging for God." I fell in love with this phrase. He compares it to "going through a drawer full of stuff, feeling around, looking for something that you are sure must be there."[20] And what I am looking for are the fingerprints of God on certain moments of my day. This causes deep gratitude as I find spiritual moments that in my haste I've blown right past. The Prayer of Examen prompts me to go back and take another look to find God.

It is never difficult to find something in my day that reflects God in a way I'd missed. Each instance I can think of reveals some quality of God that is worthy of contemplation. Never has there been a day that I've taken time to "rummage through" that I haven't found something of great value to be thankful for. Whether I've been surprised by beauty in unexpected places, or humbled by God's goodness in the face of a loved one, or inspired by creativity in something I've read—something always reveals God in the comings and goings of my day. It's a matter of taking the time to look back and reflect to find it.

Not only does it strengthen my faith to see divine attributes of God woven into my day, in and around people that l love, and through the world around me; it also hones my vision to get better at noticing the divine in all things, something that provides a deep, reassuring thrum of love and care.

Sometimes I will choose a passage of Scripture, a psalm or proverb, to read through several times. I try to leave space in between each line to listen to what the passage might be saying to me and to look for what it reveals about God. Other times, I will reflect on God by selecting a painting or piece of art and looking at it for several minutes until something comes into focus that I had not seen or noticed before. When my desire is to see or experience God, and I create space for this to happen, I am never disappointed in the outcome.

Not only does time spent in reflection on God lead me to sacred experiences of awe and wonder and gratitude, it also gives me a context for my own life and my place in the world.

Reflecting on Myself

Despite the number of times in a day that people ask me how I'm doing, this time of reflection is often the only opportunity I take to find out. *How* am *I doing?* I always need to check my pressure level, as in my PSI (pounds per square inch), that I can easily ignore during busy times. I need to stop to take my temperature to see if I'm in danger of overheating.

I use the Prayer of Examen in this part of my reflection as well. While the first part of the prayer focuses on God, the second part asks participants to focus on their own actions and behaviors. Many use this prayer at the end of the day to think back over events and decisions made, but since I can't even reflect on my *name* at the end of the day, I use this part in the mornings to look back on the day or days before.

Not only am I rummaging around for God, I am also looking at the junk in my own trunk. I need to find the stuff in the drawer that doesn't accurately reflect who I believe I am. I need to identify the ineffective ways I am relating to others as well as the inconsistencies in my actions, so that as soon as possible I can repair anything that needs to be repaired.

To do this, I continue my rummaging and I ask questions, listen for answers, and seek to make a change or repair as needed.

ASK GOOD QUESTIONS

Remember the QBQ I mentioned in chapter 2? The Question behind the Question that gets us to the best answer because it is the real question? The best way to begin to examine our own hearts is to ask the questions that take us right to our problem areas. For me, these are two good questions that bring to mind my areas of struggle:

1. Have I taken actions or made decisions that didn't represent who I see myself to be?

2. What have I been trying to control that is out of my control?

These two questions reveal my biggest issues: operating out of a false sense of self and trying to control things that are not mine to control. You will probably have different issues that require different questions. The point is not to use my questions, but to create questions that allow you to reflect on yourself and your own issues. Remember, when you can name it, you can tame it. If you can feel it, you can heal it.

A number of years ago my husband went to see a golf instructor because he thought something might be wrong with his swing. Roy brought his clubs and anticipated the instructor would want to see him hit the ball. But instead, he asked Roy a very good question, "May I see your hands?" Roy held them out and the instructor looked them over carefully on both sides. "What are you looking for?" Roy asked. The instructor pointed at a couple of spots on Roy's hands and said, "These. The callouses. They show me where you are gripping the club too tightly."

Wow. May I see your hands? The right question will take you to the right area for reflection. Where have I felt this pain before? Where have I compromised something

I believe in? Is there something underneath these feelings that I need to pay attention to?

LISTEN FOR THE WHOLE ANSWER

If I were to ask God to search my heart and see if there were any ways in me that didn't reflect the truth of who I am, it wouldn't be because *God* needs to find out what they are. It would be because I need to know! Sometimes, I already know but have pushed them away, or dismissed them or justified them without any further examination. So if I am giving God the opportunity to search my heart, or look at my hands for callouses, it is in my best interest to sit quietly and listen, without interrupting, for the answer. The whole answer.

I know from experience that either God or my brain is going to give me an answer. And I don't usually have to wait long; things come to mind pretty quickly when I ask the right questions. My mind raises its hand, so to speak, eager and ready to supply all the gory details. This is the gold I'm after, but my defense mechanisms fire up and I want to dispute or dismiss what my mind is telling me instead of listening without interrupting.

I'll share two recent experiences of listening for the whole answer.

First question: *Have I taken actions or made decisions that didn't represent who I see myself to be?*

I didn't have time to settle in to my calm chair before I heard Elliot's voice in my head repeating the question he'd asked a day earlier. "Mom, why did you yell at me in such a harsh voice?" I cringed remembering the moment. I wanted to defend myself like I had done when it had happened: "Because you were pounding your sister in the head!" I had already asked him twice to stop! I could feel the frustration rising up in me again. I knew this was what I needed to reflect on, but without the anxiety or shame that would derail me from the real answer. I kept my heart open and listening as I asked myself, *Why did you respond so harshly?* At that moment the washing machine beeped that the cycle was finished. My first thought was, *Saved by the bell!* A big part of me wanted to get up that second to go put the clothes in the dryer and wait for the answer another time. I had to tell myself, *You're right where you're supposed to be, and the clothes in the washer will still be there when you've figured out the real reason you were so harsh with Elliot. Do the kids have more need for clean clothes or for their mom to have softer responses with them?* So I stayed put, listening, and heard this answer: *You got angry because Elliot wasn't listening to you and that frustrated you. You felt out of control and you decided to show him you're the boss by yelling and making him afraid.*

Yikes. This stings as I write it here, and I feel embarrassed, but fortunately that's not all I heard. If it were, I don't think I could be sharing it here. But because I kept listening, I heard the whole answer. *But that's your old way, Nicole. That's not who you are. You have other resources to draw from now. You could have gotten him to stop in a different way that didn't involve fear or raising your voice.*

I know this is true. I know my best chance of not getting angry the next time comes in recognizing what I did and taking a closer look at why I did it. I wasn't operating out of my true heart toward my son. I took a shortcut that wasn't my way, and it didn't get me anywhere.

Here's the second question: *What have I been trying to control that is out of my control?*

This is always a good question for me, because the list is long. Many things frequently come to mind: the world, the laundry, one of the kids, the other kid, both kids, being nominated for Mother of the Year, my marriage, the neatness of my home, matching socks . . . you name it. I'm a recovering control freak. I no longer try to control everything, just most things, and I think that's progress. Two areas came to mind after asking the question and listening for the answer.

People. Little people and big people, I don't discriminate. I'm an equal opportunity controller. If people would just do what I want them to do, the way would be so much smoother for all of us! But however hard I try to create the lives I want for them, they always want to create their own! The gall. People resist being controlled, as they should, which makes my attempts to orchestrate their lives about as effective as riding my bike in the swimming pool. Having married a pilot (as in always flying by the seat of his pants) and given birth to two small pogo sticks, I'm just doomed. And I would have it no other way (well, maybe on Tuesdays) if for no other reason than the opportunity it has provided me to surrender control on a daily basis. I am learning, often the hard way, to motivate and inspire from the inside rather than control from the outside. Ugh. Is it Tuesday yet?

Plans. I really love a good, well-thought-out plan. Planned plans would probably be my love language if that were one. The only thing I like better than a good plan is a good reason to break a good plan in order to create a better plan. Unfortunately, for a good plan to work, people have to follow the plan, and that's risky. (See previous paragraph.) If no one is willing to follow it, it doesn't matter if it is the most brilliant plan on the planet. Don't ask me how I know this. Yet, I still grip too tightly to the plan itself. For example, say it's Saturday and we'd planned to go to the farmer's market and then out to eat for breakfast. And let's just say that someone in the family hasn't woken up by ten o'clock and someone else in the family gets bored and wants to play a game on the computer instead of going to breakfast, which irritates another member of the family enough to wake up the sleeping member to ask this person to get ready to follow the plan, which means that member, who sleeps like a bear in hibernation, comes roaring out of the cave claiming ignorance that there even was a plan, which causes another member of the family to start slamming things around in the kitchen! Let's just say one member of the family doesn't want to speak to any of the others because the plan that everyone had signed off on got thrown out the window. Sometimes this happens in families on Saturdays in, say, the spring.

I have to let go of the plan. Actually, I don't have to, but I choose to because what I want most isn't the plan; it is what I hope the plan will produce: connection and joy. So if skipping the farmer's market and breakfast can bring connection or joy, I have to talk myself down even though we had a good plan. *Surrender the original plan, Nicole. What good is it to be at the farmer's market with an angry family? Give up trying to control the circus and just jump on the back of the elephant and try not to be afraid.*

I used to think ducks were great examples of calm.

They look so smooth on the surface while paddling like crazy underneath. But calm is the opposite of this. Things can look out of control on the surface and still be smooth as glass on the inside. This is the kind of calm I am trying to create in my life. To do this I've had to surrender appearing in control while the world falls apart. Real calm has come from working on what is within my control, and letting go of what is not.

RESET AND REPAIR

When issues like those in the examples above come up, my homework includes making a decision about what to do with what I've learned about myself. I usually need to do some resetting or some repairing or both.

Reset

When my actions do not represent who I believe myself to be, which is more often than I'd like to admit, I need to spend some time reflecting on my identity. My actions are the litmus test of what I believe is true about me. So when I look at my actions with Elliot, I have to ask myself, do I believe that instilling fear in my child is the best way to solicit better behavior? No, I don't. More questions: Do I believe that I have to prove my worth to others? No. Am I being measured by what I wear or by how many parenting books I have read? Maybe, but is that under my control? Am I living like I believe more is better?

In the quietness of my own heart, I return to the simplest truths—my factory settings—about who I am: "I am something, but I am not everything."[21]

I am something. I came into this world as a deeply loved child of God. I was created with the *imago dei* (the image of God) imprinted in my genetic code. I was designed with a purpose and for a purpose. I have great worth and value that is mine to accept or reject. I do not have to prove this, I do not have to earn this or even maintain this; my work is to trust this with my whole heart and live from this place of trust.

When I live like I am a person of worth and value, I take better care of myself and better care of those around me. When I rest in the fact that I am loved, I am a loving mother with greater capacity. I make better choices. When I believe that I am good enough just as I am, I resist comparing myself to others. When I don't feel the need to prove my worth, I am less prone to overcommit.

But I am not everything. I hold the image of God, but I am not God. I am not a god. I am not the center of the universe or even the center of my own universe. I am a human being designed by a divine mind, created by human parents. I am reduced to tears by beauty and sacrifice, and I stand in awe of God's greatness, and I kneel because of God's goodness. There is more that I cannot control than I can control. I am not in charge of much in the larger scheme of things, but I can make much of the little I am charged with.

There are days when I feel that the weight of my responsibilities might crush me. It is on these days that I also need a hard reset of my identity. I have made too much of myself and forgotten that I am not everything. I have taken on the world and decided to run it as my own, singlehandedly.

When I realize I've done this again, I don't shrug it off carelessly. I gently set down my heavy pack, overloaded only by yours truly, and begin to sort out what pieces belong where. I remind myself that no one expected me to carry everything, and that I picked up things that didn't belong to me. I do not have to make everything work all the time for everyone. I am not holding the world together by my effort. I pick up only the things that are mine to carry, and the weight of shouldering the reasonable responsibilities of my life now feels manageable.

I am something, but I am not everything. One part

keeps the other part in perspective, working like a check and balance system inside me. When I am living too much in either part, I need to get still and reset my identity. I don't want settings I've tried to create myself or any software that I might have accidentally loaded onto my identity hardware, or even any malware that sneaked in, to define me in any way. So I reset to return to my simplest identity. I am loved and I have worth and value.

I restate this simple truth as many times as it takes to drown out the voices and restore my identity. Negative, shaming voices are not allowed in my wonderful place of safety, strength, and beauty. After all, it's my room now and I get to make the rules.

I am something, thank God, but I am not everything, thank God.

Repair

Repair work isn't really homework, because it doesn't take place in our room, but deciding how to repair a relationship does, so I'm including it here.

By the end of my reflection time, I know what I need to do, but I still take time to write it down. This accountability of writing down the plan is important for two reasons. The first is that it's easy to skip the repair work because no one but me knows it needs to be done. If I've said yes to something out of reasons inconsistent with my values, there are times I can take it as a lesson learned and let it go. But sometimes I have to, ugh, explain regretfully that I am not able to do what I've said I would. Either way, I need to spend time thinking through how I will respond differently going forward so I don't put myself in the same situation again. The second reason I need to write it down is because I am a procrastinator. It's not that I intend to skip it. I intend to do it later when I believe I will have more energy or time or whatever, only to end up not having done it at all.

Repairing damaged relationships, even a little rip in a friendship, is critical for the connection and health of the relationship. Just recently, a friend and I tried to get together for coffee and had a misunderstanding over the time and day. She was at the coffee shop for thirty minutes waiting for me, and I was oblivious until later when I discovered the mistake. At that point, it didn't matter who was wrong. I felt terrible and wanted to do whatever I could to repair what I knew was a rip— even though she indicated she was fine. I didn't need an elaborate plan, but I did need to spend time writing a thoughtful note right away that communicated how badly I felt.

To finish the story of the day I was harsh with Elliot, my written plan was to sit down with him and explain that he was right; I had indeed been harsh with him. I wanted to communicate that I didn't approve of his behavior with Abigail, but that I did not need to yell at him to let him know that. I told him I was sorry and that I was wrong.

I'm happy to report that Elliot accepted my apology and even apologized to Abigail in return. We repaired the rip and made the fabric of our relationship stronger. The greatest harm to a relationship is not when it rips; it is when the rip goes unrepaired. When we acknowledge that we have acted in a way that is "less than" who we are, more likely than not, others will respond to our shortcomings with love and care.

Homework is sitting quietly in our rooms, working to bring every last piece and part of ourselves home to safety and love. It is looking at the areas in our lives that are still "prone to wander" and reaching out to them with the great news of acceptance and love. The war is over; all the soldiers we send out there to fight for our worth can come home. We can surrender illusions of control to the realities of love. As we are able to accept our acceptance, we experience peace, and the kind of calm that quiets us with love at the very center of our souls, including the places that are "less than." This means we are ready to bring calm to the outside world of crazy, because we can finally do so from our calm home inside.

PART 3

Bringing Calm to the Outside

CHAPTER 7

Boundaries

ONE TUESDAY Roy and I were having lunch in a restaurant when I excused myself to the restroom. I hadn't even locked the door to my stall when I heard a woman a couple of stalls over whisper, "Hello?" At first I thought a friend of hers must have entered the restroom, so I didn't say anything. The woman whispered again, "Hello?" Then, "Are you there?" I tentatively answered, "Yes, I'm here." I was pretty certain she needed assistance or tissue or some other personal item. "Do you need help?" I asked in a kind tone so she would sense my willingness to help. I hadn't even finished my sentence before I heard her say, much louder this time, "Hello? I'm sorry I can't hear you; I'll have to call you back!"

Mercy. She didn't need help; she needed better cell coverage in the toilet! I still can't believe it. I was trying so carefully to help a woman who wasn't even talking to me! The stall call reveals a high number on any calm-crazy scale. Life is definitely out of control if you need to catch up with people while you go to the bathroom!

Walking the long road from crazy to crisis to calm had changed me. Coming home to myself and spending time in my room doing my homework had begun to pay off. I was beginning to live from a calm center and be able to connect more and more of the dots about what had created crazy in my life for so many years.

At the same time, I feared getting pulled back into the kind of crazy I'd lived in before The Day Life Fell Apart. I wasn't worried that my center of calm would crumble. I was concerned that my life didn't have enough structure to keep the crazy from seeping back into everything. I needed new strategies to live out calm in a still crazy world. I had no illusions about bringing calm to that world, but I did hope that with some well-placed framework I could bring some calm to my home.

Having a room of my own was changing me from the inside, and I was beginning to recognize the need for some sort of room for our family. I wanted to draw an imaginary line around my family in order to create a place of calm and safety, and yes, strength and beauty. But for the life of me, I could never see our family sitting quietly together and visualizing this place. Not only would this concept not fly, they would laugh me out of the room.

I needed to set some boundaries that could protect me as well as our family from being pulled back into crazy.

In 1999, Drs. Henry Cloud and John Townsend wrote *Boundaries*, a groundbreaking book for relationships. *Boundaries* taught many of us how to set healthy limits in every kind of relationship. Still today, if you need help drawing lines to stop the crazy of unhealthy relationships, reading *Boundaries* is the perfect place to start. But when it came to creating calm, I wasn't struggling with relationships; I was wrestling with things like scheduling and overcommitment.

I needed to put boundaries around things like technology and work in order to help me control my time and commitments. And I wanted to draw boundaries that would protect the relationships within our family, which meant setting limits on screens and too many after-school activities. I didn't want to take anything away from anyone; I wanted to put up healthy borders so we could enjoy these things properly. Using the imaginary dotted lines explained in *Boundaries*, I began to draw around a few areas that could take over unless there were limits in place.

SETTING BOUNDARIES AROUND THE USE OF TECHNOLOGY

Our dependence on technology can be crazy-making and our capacity for multitasking endless. Tech companies do not mind this, especially as our dependence on their products increases earnings and market share. Many people have been trying to sound the alarm for years, but it doesn't appear to be working on a large scale. Our devices are more popular than ever and more ingrained in our lives than we realize.

This was certainly true for me, but seeing this become true in the lives of our kids prompted me to do something about it.

I began to notice them going from one screen to the next. As soon as they laid down one device, they would quickly pick up another. I realized I couldn't get upset with the kids for their nonstop use of technology unless I was modeling good limits on my own tech use. I know, it pretty much stinks that a double standard doesn't work.

For years I have allowed computer time to bleed over into other areas, leeching time away from walking or reading or being still and quiet. I've actually thought, *Why don't I have as much time as I used to?* Guess what? I do. I have always had twenty-four hours in a day. I have as much or as little time as I've ever had, but I have lost my sense of time by not setting boundaries with technology.

When I thought about what healthy use of technology might look like for me and what limits I needed to set, these are the ones that came up first. I'm not doing them perfectly, but I am doing them regularly.

Turn off email when engaged in something else. When I turn off the email program on my laptop, I can think of it more like my outside mailbox. There may be mail there because I heard the carrier outside, but I'll go and get it when I'm dressed and ready to do something with it. Since email requires none of that getting dressed stuff or even having to walk outside, I have a tendency to let it spill all over the place and gobble up all my time. I find myself looking at email at times when I can't do anything with it, which may be the biggest time waster ever, because I will have to look at it again when I am going to deal with it properly. I'm much better at setting boundaries with snail mail, probably because it doesn't beep and pile up every two minutes!

While I cannot control how often people send me email, I can control how often I look at it and when I respond to it. I do not have to give my attention to email just because it clamors for it or because everyone else seems to devote the day to it. When my children yell for me to come and see the biggest spit bubble ever, but I'm in the middle of something, I do not respond immediately to their request. "I'm cutting up fruit, sweetie. When I finish, I'll come." I know the bubble will probably be gone, but that's a chance I'm willing to take. I want to give my children my attention when I am able to give it as completely and freely as possible. Who wants a frustrated mother who comes and rolls her eyes at the biggest spit bubble ever? No one.

I am not strong enough to be working on my computer and not look at my email as it comes in, but I am strong enough to turn off the email program so I can pay attention to what I'm paying attention to. I cannot live in calm if I'm trying to squeeze living, working, mothering, and connecting with people in between emails that will never stop coming. But when I turn off my email, even for a few hours, I am free from those demands and free to concentrate, to play, to rest, to shop—whatever I am choosing to give my full attention to.

A beautiful byproduct of setting limits on the reach

of my email is that I inadvertently created time for myself. I discovered while writing one afternoon when my email was off that not only was my concentration better, but I got work done in much less time. I didn't fully make the connection that day, but after a few times I knew I'd been more effective, and also more efficient. Whenever a project takes longer than the time allotted, it causes me to scramble, moving things around to give myself more time, creating crazy. But with a secure boundary around this huge time waster, I was finishing within my estimated time and sometimes even early. Who knew I could do more if I wasn't distracted twenty times after I'd begun?

Mute alerts, alarms, and ringers. Whenever a text alert comes from my phone, it startles me a little, *and where is my phone anyway?* I find it hard not to stop or interrupt what I'm doing and check my phone. Why is that? It's because our brains get a little shot of dopamine (its favorite drug) whenever we hear that ding. *Something has happened! Someone's trying to reach me! My lives are refilled for Candy Crush! Come quick!* But if I don't hear those rings and alerts, they don't distract me. Much like turning off my email, muting all the alerts provides me the freedom to concentrate on whatever I am trying to concentrate on.

This boundary keeps those pesky, nonstop alerts from physically changing my brain. I am more able to embody calm when I am not getting dopamine surges every few minutes. Our brains are dopamine addicts, and my phone had become my dealer. During the first few weeks of putting my phone on silent, I would forget I had done it and my brain would start to wonder, *Why isn't anyone texting me? I'd better go check my phone.* I would remember I'd put it on silent and congratulate myself for getting clean. It felt so good that I could call the shots (literally) regarding the dopamine, and not my dealer, um, phone.

You might be saying to yourself, *What if a text is critical? It could be something really important.* It isn't. If I'm waiting for a critical text, I do leave my phone on. When I am out for the evening and there is a sitter with my children, I don't turn my phone to silent. When I am waiting to hear the results of a friend's MRI, my phone is on. But for the most part, the text messages and calls I receive are not critical, unless you count as critical someone needing the recipe for Picnic Potato Salad.

When I am having family time, or quiet time, or just goof-off time, I want to be fully present. I don't want to interrupt that time for what might be happening somewhere else. If I don't set this boundary, my phone brings distraction opportunities twenty-four hours a day. I can't function like this, and not because I don't like smartphones or because I resist technological advances. It is because I no longer want to live in crazy, and constant distractions create crazy. An old German proverb applies here: "You can't stop the birds from flying over your head, but you can keep them from building a nest in your hair!"[22]

I keep my devices quiet to limit the disruptions they inevitably cause and also to model control for my kids. If I am okay with their being on their phones all the time (when they actually get them—at age thirty!) then I can be on my phone all the time. But if I want my kids to know a different way, a way they might not appreciate for a long time, one that cultivates their creativity and shores up their concentration and allows them to work more efficiently, then I have to stay off my phone. I have to model the kind of control I want my kids to exhibit, and lead the way in setting limits on some things to make space for the things we love most, like each other.

I still forget to do this at times, because with the number of devices I have, it seems like it takes an hour to make sure everything is on silent, but when I mute the bells and whistles, I feel calm coming in like a breeze off the ocean. I feel in control of my technology versus feeling like the technology is controlling me.

Take sabbaticals from social media. Are you familiar with the term *FOMO*? The letters stand for Fear of Missing Out. Someone coined this phrase to give words to the fear and anxiety that we might be missing out on something. Magazine ads compete to create FOMO so we'll buy the clothes that show we're "in the know." Who doesn't want to be invited to *the* party? We don't want to miss out or be left out of anything, especially something we want to be included in. This desire is so normal and human. I remember feeling FOMO every single day of junior high. As social beings, we want to experience what others are experiencing; we want to belong.

Through the creation of Facebook and the like, FOMO has become an epidemic. Every single hour of every single day it is possible to open your computer and see a hundred or more things you are missing out on! Our friends all over the country are doing amazing things and going fabulous places (yay, them!), but, hmm, without us (ugh). I've never seen anyone post a vacation photo looking sad that I'm not there (but a cool idea!). FOMO could also stand for Facebook Only Makes Outsiders! It's hard on the psyche to see photos of happy, tanned people on vacation if I'm stuck at home with kids and the stomach flu. I am *not* bashing social media—well, not completely. I'm simply advocating drawing a boundary around it to protect our emotional health. We can do this by giving social media more realistic context in our lives.

Research has revealed a connection between the high usage of social media and depression.[23] The reasons are not surprising. Social media heightens depression because of comparison, which you may recall from chapter 1 was one of the ingredients that created crazy in my life. We look from the outside at other people's lives and we rank ourselves in ways that lead to discontent. Remember, comparison never reveals the whole story, only as much of the story as we need to feel inferior. Every comparison we make is like a dry twig, and before long we have a dangerous pile of kindling in the middle of our living room. One spark, which social media is happy to deliver, will start the fire that burns up satisfaction and gratitude faster than we can click "like."

Facebook cleverly creates the illusion that we are connecting and participating in the lives of others simply by looking at their posts. But that's not participation. We are not engaged with most of our Facebook "friends" on a relational level unless we spend time with them in person. We are merely spectators who can look at the lives of others and leave comments.

Fortunately, Facebook hasn't been a habit for me, so consuming less has not been difficult. I've never liked the way it tries to connect me to other people. While I'm trying to decipher how Facebook connected me to some guy named Albert across the country who knows three of my sister's friends in Alabama, an hour has gone by and I have no idea where it went. However, I now know that Charlene's dog died yesterday, Mary's daughter went to the prom with a really goofy-looking boy, Sarah got engaged at the Arboretum, and Michael, an old friend from high school, bought a new truck. I feel awful. Not because I feel left out, but because I feel overwhelmed that I can't keep up with all the relationships I'm not really in. *Should I send a card to Charlene? Or just post a couple of sentences? I'll have to get a gift for Sarah, but she didn't exactly tell me about her engagement, so should I wait for the announcement or like her pictures? Thank goodness I don't need to send a gift to Michael for getting a new truck!*

Social media is simply that—media. It is not possible to have five hundred friends. It is possible to have five hundred people's posts to look through, but I can barely keep up with the people that live under my roof! So even trying to stay current on people's posts creates crazy, never mind trying to post something about yourself! Especially if you feel like I do that stress comes from what you're *not* getting done.

If you are trying to create calm in your life, take a sabbatical from social media. Come up with a schedule that lets you detox and get a break, such as, three weeks on and then one week off. Be wise and intentional about the amount of usage and always remind yourself that looking at other people's lives from the outside is depressing.

Technology brings information, photos, apps, even movies, right to our fingertips. The possibilities are endless and conveniences are practical. But technology asks for a lot in return: our attention, our information, our choices, our focus, and our time. Facebook, Instagram, and the like are businesses that seek to make a profit off of our connections. They sell our information, analyze our habits, capitalize on our usage, and try to connect with our friends (without us!). I use social media most wisely when I make conscious choices about what I'm willing to give away and what I'm not.

SETTING BOUNDARIES AROUND WORK

Most of my adult life I've had an office in my home. For decades this provided the ultimate convenience and allowed me to be more available than if I had to go to an office. But it also created an unhealthy relationship with work. If I wanted to go to work at four in the morning, or until four in the morning, I could. Even after having kids, while it was much harder to work in general, working from home still made this kind of crazy schedule possible. Mostly because I could use bits of family time to catch up on calls or answer a few emails.

This worked well until everyone I worked with also started working from home. Even people who had an office to go to during the day were now staying home or bringing their laptops home from the office to work in the evenings! What had been convenient for me and provided a little extra time when I needed to catch up became *de rigueur* for a large segment of the population. Suddenly, it seemed as though everyone was working from everywhere every hour of the day. No one sets work hours anymore. People take working vacations and make themselves available 24/7. No one is really off, even on the weekends. The closest I see to off is an out-of-office email, but that is simply to adjust expectations of when the busy recipient might get back to you. Often this out-of-office response doesn't mean someone isn't working; it indicates he or she is working on something else or working somewhere else. We are never *not* working.

I appreciate the expectation adjustment that an out-of-office reply provides. I'd like to create a permanent one! I sense people get bothered when I'm not immediately available to them. Maybe they think, *You aren't supposed to be in charge of your own time when I'm not free to be in charge of mine! How can you be off when I need something?* This nonexistent line can cause crazy, so I needed to draw a new line around work. If I waited to take a break until everything was finished, I'd never take a break, because my work is never finished. If I don't set limits on work and also take time off, my every waking moment will be filled with work to be done.

This can't be good for our psyches. It can't be good for anything really, except productivity, and I'm not convinced it's all that good for that. There is an ad on the back of a bus-stop bench in our area that reads, "All work and no play makes Frank a very good realtor." How sad! Not only because Frank thinks this is true, but because of the underlying message that Frank is only a good realtor if he isn't doing anything but real estate. Why can't Frank be a good realtor and have a life? Are the two things mutually exclusive? I guess Frank thinks they are.

With the exception of writing this book (authentic disclosure) I limit the hours I work in a day to about six or seven. Not because I can get all my work done in that amount of time, but because after that amount of time, I am choosing to stop. I realize I am able to do this because I work for myself, but at this season in my life I would try to do it this way even if I wasn't self-employed. Thirty-five hours a week is a full-time job and I want time to do other things. This decision affects my income just as it would anyone else's, but so many of life's best choices are made by doing what you believe to be right for you. In my case, I'm choosing based on what will create more calm and allow me to live in a way that reflects what I value. I can't expect my priorities to stay priorities for long if I'm not making the choices that support them. My children will think I work all the time if that's all they see me doing. Especially when I have a choice in the matter. Many men and women don't have a choice, and that is a different issue, but for many who do, setting a boundary that reflects your priorities is critical.

So there are times in the day when I am not available for work. I close the door to my office and do my best to leave work there. I keep school papers and other records in my office, so I might go in to get something, but I don't stay. If I'm successful, I don't return to my office until the following morning. Do I need to tell you how present I can be with whatever is going on in the house when I close the door to my office? The value of *being present* is enormous. Whether I'm spending time with the kids, or Roy, or even doing dishes in the kitchen, it seems as though giving my full attention to it makes it so much more satisfying.

Don't think I'm not tempted to say to myself, *They're fine,* and slip down the hall to do a little work. But it's a trap! I know this because I've done it. One thing leads to another, and then I've been in my office for forty-five minutes. I have to resist going back to the office even when everyone else is doing their own thing and no one needs anything, because it's not just about them. I need the boundary around work to keep the unhealthy pull of "public productivity" in check. I need to engage in private productivity, like coloring or putting together a puzzle or just playing alongside the kids.

I'm not doing this perfectly, or anywhere close to it, but I am putting limits on work. Again, I don't think I'm seeking to do this simply because I am self-employed with kids. If I were working nine or ten hours a day for a company, I would do the work but fiercely set limits on anything over ten. I would put a lot of words around Mommy's work time to help the kids value it, and I'd make sure to be as fully engaged as possible when not at work. I also believe, and this is a little harder to imagine, that even if I were single with no kids, I would try to set limits to the amount of work I choose to do in the day. It's just a healthy thing to do.

Not only do I set limits on our technology and my work time, I also create extra buffers as added security, because even with boundaries in place, crazy can still flood the borders. It can spill over walls and cause chaos. Our family life is too important to allow it to be washed away by crazy.

SETTING BOUNDARIES AROUND FAMILY TIME

When I was little, my family lived for several years in Pensacola, Florida. I remember spending hours at the beach building sandcastles of varying magnitude. It was my favorite beach activity, even more than swimming in the ocean, especially during seaweed season. I would estimate that I built a hundred or more sandcastles in my construction days. If these sandcastles taught me anything, it was to include a deep moat around the castle. This moat is essential to keep the castle from washing away the first time the water comes roaring up.

A large part of keeping crazy under control is counting on it to come roaring up, just like the tide. We are never free of the threat of crazy rushing in to wash away large parts of the calm we've created. Stuff happens that is out of our control, in good ways and bad. We are delighted when friends stop by with their new dog and we drop everything to play, but not so much when an important school event that didn't make it onto the calendar takes the evening we had planned at home. Family moats are what I call the boundaries I've set to protect the time we spend together as a family. They do not keep out all the crazy, but they do slow it down, giving us time to adjust to the rush of crazy without getting soaked.

These are a few boundaries that function as family moats around our house.

No screens at the dinner table. Dinner time is pretty sacred for us. We don't have dinner as a family every night of the week, so it's a special and important space when we all get around the table. This moat protects that time for our family to talk to each other about our lives, to engage with each other in meaningful ways. Even if we've been "screened" all day for whatever reason—sickness or vacation or those days when Mommy is working on her book—the overflow of crazy isn't likely to wash us away because of this moat. We can talk about anything, and do, because the TV can't break in, our phones are on silent, and our electronics are turned off. This allows us to argue about the quality of the chicken nuggets with nothing to distract us!

Evenings at home. One night a week Roy and I have a date night and we are usually out another night due to an obligation or commitment, perhaps a party or a school function. We both try to be home the other five nights. This is not always possible, but here is why it is critical: Things go differently when I am home than when I am away or out for the evening. It's not that the kids go to bed too late or eat too much dessert when they have a babysitter—that can happen when I'm home. It's the next morning that is the problem.

When I haven't thought through the next day before heading out for the evening, and I usually haven't, as I'm busy still solving the problems of *that* day, then at 6:30 the next morning, I'm in trouble. I know from experience that when I'm in trouble at 6:30 in the morning, I'm still going to be in trouble at 6:30 in the evening! So too many nights out late, followed by challenging mornings of being too tired and too unprepared, followed by too much responsibility in the day, creates too much pressure, and I'm right back in the crazy soup. I'm always astounded how one off-schedule night creates an off-schedule week. And that off-schedule week easily begets another week of feeling behind. If two weeks pass like this, we've embarked on a pattern of irritable mornings and power struggles in the afternoon, which means everything is harder than it should be. So when my social or work calendar starts to flood its banks, the evenings-at-home moat kicks in to catch the crazy and keep our family safe and dry.

View *no* as a family word. *No* is a moat-building word. It is a word that helps us dig deep enough to create a real buffer against all the crazy that comes at us as a family. *No* is also a family word, because one person can't dig fast enough to create a family moat on their own. Before we created this moat, craziness would sneak into our family when a kid said yes to a play date without checking in, or Roy would commit to a meeting not realizing it fell on the night we were going to watch a movie as a family.

To dig this moat, we decided to make weekly schedules that everyone in the family has input into creating. For example, if we schedule a movie night, then each of us has to say no to other things in order to protect our time together. Roy may have to say no to a game on television, I might have to say no to meeting a friend for dinner, and the kids might have to say no to being on their electronics. The kids are much better at respecting this moat when they have helped to create it around things they enjoy. We are learning to use no as a family word to create the yes we want to experience together.

It is not easy work for four people to work out a schedule. In the past when it seemed too hard, we just didn't do it, or tried and gave up and the crazy flooded in. Our good intentions were washed away and then nothing replaced them except frustration. We all knew this wasn't the way.

Recently, this "No Is a Family Word" moat meant that our kids had to choose only one sport they wanted to play that required practice outside of school ("Mom! Really?"). We came to an agreement together that more than one sport for each, two total, would require too much time in the car right after school (which neither child likes). Since making that decision and getting into the routine with the other activities we want to do as well, we have affirmed it as a good decision for all of us. Our kids are coming to understand, as we are as well, in a deeper way, that no can be a positive word when used to bring us closer to what we value. For example, we now have more time to spend with friends after school. Our moat is creating structure around our family (and friends) time, and we are all feeling better about the consistency and the calm that has come with it. We are learning to compromise our individual needs/wants for the sake of our collective. We are more than four people trying to work out a schedule. We are a family working together to create what we value, and learning together how to protect it.

If you don't have children, you can adapt these ideas to dig moats that will help you protect what you value and to serve as an extra buffer that will keep your "room" safe and dry. *No* is not a bad word, and we don't need to be afraid to say it, especially when it offers protection and creates a boundary around something we love and value, like our own souls.

My friend Carla is single and learning to use the word *no* as a boundary to protect her evenings at home. For years, Carla thought she didn't have reasons to say no, like her married friends or those with kids, so she ended up saying yes to things she would have preferred to decline. She didn't have to be home at a certain time or have to coordinate with anyone else's schedule, so people assumed she was free to do whatever anyone asked her to do. Carla was overcommitted and resentful toward others, because she never thought she could say no without a "legitimate" reason. It turns out Carla had forgotten the most legitimate of all: herself! She began to protect the most important person in her life from the feeling that she was tagging along or had been included because she was available. Carla came to discover that she loved being home and didn't feel nearly as lonely as she feared she would. She trusted she didn't have to have any specific conflict in order to say *no*. She could choose when participating sounded like fun and not be pulled into situations that would make her feel uncomfortable or unwanted.

Whether it is setting limits to keep from working too much or paying closer attention to the time we all spend on devices, boundaries and moats can provide us with the opportunity to enjoy quality time in a less crazy environment.

My goal in sharing some of the boundaries I'm drawing is to inspire and support you in creating your own boundaries to protect the things you truly value. Most likely your moats will be different from mine. Boundaries are not rules and even a moat will not keep all the crazy outside your castle. Life is unique to each of us and our circumstances are too individual to draw hard lines or make rigid rules that should apply to all. In fact, some of that rigidity is how I got to crazy in the first place. However, acknowledging there is no one grand set of boundaries does not mean we have to accept all kinds of crazy just because our circumstances are unique. For me, setting boundaries to limit the reach of the crazy was an important step in extending calm to my family. It also revealed the way we could grow together in our understanding of calm and in our strategies to create it as a family.

CHAPTER 8

Keys

CRAZY COMES in all shapes and sizes and enters into our lives wherever it can gain a foothold. Every marriage, every friendship, every parent-child relationship, every professional relationship—every relationship—runs the risk of getting sidetracked by crazy. Every responsibility, from leadership to laundry, can be affected and infected by crazy. Lately, events on the world stage, such as elections and economic summits, have left no doubt in my mind that the world has accepted crazy as the new normal. So many circumstances and outcomes *are* out of control, as well as out of *my* control, but this leaves me feeling helpless and powerless.

Having given calm and crazy the lion's share of my

thinking over the last many years, I can say this with confidence: *the only answer to crazy is calm*. Regardless of the form or the arena in which it reigns, crazy is crazy and calm is always the antidote. Just as responding to hate with more hate multiplies the hate, responding to crazy in crazy ways just reproduces more crazy. I realize even the word *crazy* is subjective, and that what may seem crazy and out of control to me might not seem crazy to you at all. Fortunately, this is not an issue since calm is always the solution for whatever kind of crazy we are trying to counter in our lives.

The gravest danger we ever face from crazy is not recognizing it for what it is. But to recognize the crazy, especially when it is in us, gives us the opportunity to counter it with calm in the very place it occurs. As the following fictional story portrays, when we create calm inside ourselves, we reproduce calm in our relationships, communities, and even in the world around us.

The conversation was going nowhere. The kids were away at a friend's house and the Coopers were locked in an old argument they could practically have in their sleep. Almost on cue, the conversation in the kitchen began to heat up as Sarah worked to clean up the day's mess. "You never do anything around the house to help me," Sarah voiced to her husband, Michael.

"I'm doing other stuff, Sarah, you know that. I'm working extra hours, I'm paying the bills."

"I'm sure you could take out the trash or unload the dishwasher without putting us in a financial crisis."

"I do take out the trash!" Michael objected. "Stop acting like I don't do *anything* around here!"

Sarah paused, feeling a little guilty about what she was about to say, but she decided to say it anyway: "You *don't* do anything around here."

Michael got up from the table to go to the family room, almost successful in ignoring Sarah's insult, but then he decided on a parting shot: "If you'd stop spending so much, I wouldn't have to work so hard!" He left the room.

"Oh brother," said Sarah, all guilt gone, dropping the gloves and raising her voice: "I don't spend a quarter of what you spend on all the electronics we 'need'!"

"Maybe you should go back to work, Sarah. Then you wouldn't have time to sit around getting bitter about all the stuff I'm doing or not doing!"

That stung. *This is crazy*, she thought.

Sarah's adrenaline was high, her heart was beating

fast, and she had her comeback ready to go. *I should go back to work and then I could hire someone to do all the things you said you would do!* She wanted to say it to hurt Michael because she was hurt, but that would continue the crazy. It would only make things worse. She knew this from the ten times they'd had this argument before. Still, she felt the tears coming.

She was so frustrated. What would it take for him to see she needed more help? Instead of following him into the family room to deliver her comeback, Sarah sat down at the kitchen table to take a deep breath and let the tears come. She needed to think, but she was too tired to do it clearly. She felt embarrassed. She knew she'd brought this on herself.

She had started it when she'd said, "You never do anything around the house to help me." She could have said, "Michael, I need your help. Would you unload the dishwasher tonight while I clear the table?" If he had come back with some snarky comment, then the argument would have been his fault, but he didn't and it was hers. She was feeling overwhelmed and she wanted him to get a taste of what she was feeling, but there was a better way, and Sarah knew she had not chosen it, again.

She'd let weariness get the best of her. She did need Michael's help. But instead of asking specifically for what she needed, she had criticized him for doing nothing. She knew that when she was this tired, she didn't choose her words carefully. They finally had part of an evening at home while the kids were at their friends' homes, and instead of enjoying it, it had been hijacked by crazy. Now what?

Sarah made an intentional and difficult choice. Instead of giving in to anger, she decided to try to calm down. It was an experiment, but she knew getting angry didn't work, so she had nothing to lose. She walked humbly into the living room. "I'm sorry, Michael. I'm feeling overwhelmed and I took it out on you. Can we table this discussion for now? I would still like to talk about it, but can we pick it up later when I'm not so tired?"

Michael immediately softened. "I'm sorry, Sarah, I know you're under a lot of stress because I have been working so much. But I can help more going forward."

"I just let myself get too tired. I didn't pick the right time or way to talk about this. I need to give myself a time-out. Can we revisit this tomorrow when I'm in a better place?"

"Of course, Sarah. I'm sorry."

When Sarah came back to the kitchen about forty-five minutes later, she was ready to engage again. She knew Michael had gone out to pick up the kids, which was a big help, and now they were back in the family room playing a game on the Wii. The dishes were still piled up in the sink, and the trash had not been taken out, but Sarah did not feel angry. She'd taken the time to do the things that brought calm to the center of her soul, and she felt a whole lot better.

Sarah returned to the scene of the crazy without any of the crazy returning with her.

Sarah did several things to unlock calm and diffuse crazy in her relationship with Michael. The choices she made are important keys to unlocking calm in our *relationships*.

- Key: *Sense* where the crazy is coming from
- Key: *Send* yourself to your room
- Key: *Strike* while the iron is cold

The more we use these keys in the midst of crazy, the more we can live in relational calm. It helps me to remember things when I create visuals to support them. I have put these three keys on a mental keychain and call them my "calm keys." Because calm lives in me, these keys help me turn things around when they are heading toward crazy.

Let's take a closer look at each key and how we can use it to help unlock calm and diffuse crazy.

KEY: SENSE WHERE THE CRAZY IS COMING FROM

Sarah used this key when she recognized she was the one creating crazy instead of calm. She recognized that part of the crazy was due to her feeling tired and over-whelmed, and that because of this she hadn't chosen her words wisely. It takes a calm center to be able to realize this. This ability comes from doing our homework and using what we are learning about ourselves.

There are days right around dinnertime when I'm pretty sure someone secretly injected my children with high-fructose corn syrup, just to mess with me. They are running around, throwing things, and chasing each other; that is, until one trips. The chasing stops and the screaming starts. One evening in particular, I had been trying desperately to finish one email and get dinner on the table, and "Can't you two settle down a little, please?" And then it hits me. I am frazzled. I am sensing crazy from every direction, but the biggest wave is coming from me! In trying to get a little work done after hours, the kids' crazy was driving me crazy. I was the one with exposed nerve endings!

So instead of getting frustrated with them, I close my computer and turn off my phone and put dinner on simmer. I take the kids into the back yard and watch them jump on the trampoline for a bit. I resume fixing dinner (and regulating internally), and by the time the family sits down to eat, things are much calmer.

If we can sense where the crazy is coming from, we stand the best chance of bringing some calm to it. It is worth noting that this becomes trickier when you sense the crazy is coming from someone else. It doesn't usually help to point it out to that person. Hopefully you can take my word for this.

There have been times I have sensed the craziness was coming from Roy. I remember one evening, he was excited to watch a football game and had also offered to make dinner before the game. I was excited to let him! A few mishaps occurred that were out of his control and necessitated an impromptu trip to the grocery and a second impromptu trip for propane. By the time dinner was ready, he'd missed the first half of the game! His frustration was, um, high. When one of the kids refused to eat the dinner Roy had made and asked if he would make something else, not only could I sense where the crazy was coming from, the neighbor three blocks away could have sensed it! I suggested calmly that we all thank

Daddy for making dinner and excuse him to his room to eat and watch the second half of the game with some peace and quiet. This was the key to creating calm and it also kept a small child alive to see another sunrise.

KEY: SEND YOURSELF TO YOUR ROOM

In the story of the Coopers, Sarah recognized that no good decisions would be made in the middle of crazy, so she sent herself to her room. She gave herself a time-out. She needed space and time to downshift out of angry and transition to calm.

In the story I just told about Roy, I suggested he take a time-out. I wasn't sending him to his room; I was sensing his need for a break and freeing him up to go. When I sense the crazy is coming from me—like Sarah, I send myself to my room. I know that in doing this, I am caring for myself and I'm caring for others. I'm putting on my oxygen mask first.

Every time I am on a flight, the attendant giving the preflight safety briefing always includes some form of this statement, "Should the cabin pressure fall below normal, oxygen masks will drop from the ceiling. Put your mask over your nose and mouth and begin to breathe normally. Be sure to put your mask on *before* helping those around you." It dawned on me a few years ago that the flight attendants were really talking to the women on the plane. They have to remind us again and again—help yourself before you try to help those around you—because it's not our way! But when it comes to oxygen, we have to make it our way or we won't be helping anyone.

This is why we must learn to send ourselves to our room, not to withdraw from others but to recharge and replenish when we are depleted. It's like putting on our oxygen mask first. This is not being selfish; it's the opposite. When I don't take care of myself, I'm not able to take care of those around me. So when I sense the crazy happening (like the cabin pressure dropping), I send myself to my room (to put on my mask) so I can keep breathing in order to help those around me breathe as well.

When things get crazy with the kids and I'm overheating, they know I will send myself to my room. They'll hear me say something like, "I will be back in ten minutes or so; I need to take a little break and catch my breath." They usually respond well to this, but not always. Sometimes when they have been nipping at my heels to get some toy, I might hold up my hand and say, "Wait! Please, I need to spend a few minutes in my room." They follow me.

"But Moooomm!"

I am gently closing the door. "If you need an answer right now, it will be no, but if you can wait ten minutes, we can discuss it more."

They rarely mind waiting.

In the afternoons, I will often send myself to my room for a quick nap. If I wait too long, sometimes Roy will suggest it. He knows it is self-care and care for the family. I'm no good without a nap. Really. I become a snapping turtle at best; at worst I'm a female spider looking to bite someone's head off! But when I take care of myself, I make life better and safer for everyone. I want to be rested when the kids come running into the house, lunch boxes empty and arms full of things they've created at school. I want to be refreshed when Roy tells me he's booked a three-day golf trip for the next week.

This key is permission to send myself to my room before anyone else wants to send me there.

KEY: STRIKE WHILE THE IRON IS COLD

Sarah used a technique that was passed on to me by Dr. Ryan Davis in Santa Monica.[24] It is sage wisdom from a professional psychiatrist who has helped many people create calm. To create the best chance of getting the results you want, he advises people to "strike while the iron is cold"! The first time he said it, I laughed out loud. I wasn't expecting the cold part. But his words have been a powerful tool in creating calm in my life. When Sarah chose to put the argument with Michael on hold until they weren't angry at each other, she wasn't giving up on getting more help around the house. She was choosing to discuss it with him when she could articulate it from a place of calm, not when she felt overwhelmed and anxious. From my experience, this means she will have a much better chance of actually getting what she needs from Michael.

For the record, this advice does not mean striking someone with a cold iron! It means using restraint "in the moment" to allow intense emotions to calm down before trying to have a productive discussion. When emotions are high, the brain is flooded and cannot function at its designed capacity. Nothing gets solved, accomplished, worked out, figured out, or sorted out when people are yelling or not in control of their emotions. Sometimes striking while the iron is cold means waiting until the next day or the next week to bring up a topic that has been fraught with emotion.

In one recent example of this, Roy was planning to take the kids out for dinner to give me a couple of hours to myself. He'd been away all day in meetings and knew I could use a break. He said he would come home and pick up the kids at 5:45, if I would have them ready. I was grateful for the windfall of time and was already planning what I would do with it. I got the kids dressed and they put on their socks and shoes, and then they got on their iPads to wait for Daddy. Well, Daddy was running a little late, and when he got home to pick them up, the kids were in the middle of games on their iPads that they wanted to finish before leaving. Understandably, Roy said no, and both kids got upset. Roy got very frustrated with me because he didn't think the kids were ready if they were still on their iPads. I got frustrated with Roy because ready in my mind meant dressed with socks and shoes, not waiting outside on the driveway. Clearly there was a misunderstanding in our house around the word *ready*.

As he became more and more frustrated, Roy said to me, "I want to talk about the kids and their computer time!" I said, "Absolutely . . . but not tonight." This was not the time to make a new rule. At a hot moment like we were in, it wouldn't have surprised me if Roy had ordered me to dismantle the kids' devices piece by piece. I completely understood his frustration, but the right policy for doing it differently would not be forthcoming in these moments. As it turned out, we discussed the issue the next day, calmly, and came up with some new boundaries and a new definition of the word *ready* that has already served us well.

This is a very effective key to use with my kids as well. When I say no or ask for their cooperation or participation, they don't always respond positively. As a result, I've had to accept that sometimes they feel like I'm a mean mom, or that they hate me, or even that they want to run away from home and find better parents. Regardless of what they are telling me, I almost always choose to strike when the iron is cold. It is amazing the difference a day makes. The following morning, if I say, "Elliot, can we talk about the words you chose yesterday when you were upset?" I don't even have to repeat them to him before he says, "Mom, I'm sorry. I was angry you said no, but I didn't mean it when I said I hated you." Whew. That's what striking when the iron is cold can do. If I had engaged with his words at the time he was saying them and told him they weren't true, he would have assured me they were and offered me proof! I don't want that. When kids get flooded with emotions they say things they don't mean; we all do, and the key to calm in this kind of relational crazy is to strike while the iron is cold.

In the top drawer of my desk I have the key to an old post office box, a key to a bicycle lock that is broken, and a spare key to a house we live in. I don't need these keys, which is why they are strewn about in my desk drawer. The keys I need are the ones I use most often and they are on my key ring. This is where my Calm Keys are now. I took those three keys that don't unlock anything nearly as important as calm and labeled them with Sense, Send, and Strike. They can't open the front door of the house or start the car, but in relationships they can open the door to calm communication or start a conversation in the right way, which unlocks exactly what the front door does: the safety and calm of home.

CHAPTER 9

Calm

MY PARTICULAR RECIPE for crazy was made up of five key ingredients: distraction, multitasking, overcommitment, comparison, and pressure. In the years leading up to my crisis, these seemed to be the elements most responsible for creating the crazy in my life. Somehow, combined with my personal issues, they turned me inside out and every which way but calm. So it would make sense for me to completely avoid each of these in the future. That would ensure that I could live in calm from here forward, right? Unfortunately, these are common ingredients for us all and have been staples in the kitchen of my life for decades. They have always been on hand to create crazy and they probably always will be.

For example, while I don't see distraction disappearing completely from my pantry, I do want to shove it to the back of the top shelf. While I don't think I will ever be able to fully stop comparing myself, I can work to recognize when I'm doing it and make a different choice if I am stocked up with other "go to" ingredients that won't create crazy.

From my created center of calm, I am reducing and replacing the five ingredients that hold the most potency to create crazy. I've discovered that when I use a new ingredient, it creates something different than what I'd made before! (Duh!) Cutting down and replacing the things that create crazy is helping me maintain a higher level of calm.

REDUCE: Distraction
REPLACE WITH: Focused Attention

When the kids were little, a friend gave me a piece of advice. You might remember how I feel about advice, but this piece made sense to me at the time. She knew enough about me to know I am a fairly focused person, and she seemed to like me anyway. One day we were at the park with my son and her two kids who were toddlers, when she sighed and said, "Start now making peace with distractions." She said this as she left our conversation to help one of her boys who was calling for her. I remember thinking that it was good advice for me because I'd always been at war with distractions. She came back to the conversation and I told her I'd start working on the peace treaty. We laughed and I knew she was right, but I didn't know how right. I've already shared how I did learn to make peace and gave in to living distracted from morning to night. A pinball had nothing on me! I not only made peace with distractions; many of them became my best friends!

Some days I feel as though I'm still too friendly with distractions. When I've spent my entire day putting out fires (that probably would have burned out on their own), I feel as though the kids got what they needed, and all I got was distracted. I know this is part of the work of parenting, and when my kids were younger and unable to comprehend that I also needed to use the restroom, I understood and accepted this. They weren't old enough to realize that the lack of significant focused time, with the exception of being in the bathroom, would take an already divided attention span and divide it again, then again, then again. By 2011, I had 653 attention spans.

But after both of my kids started school I had to work hard at reducing distraction and bringing my divided attention spans into unity. I wanted to strengthen my ability to concentrate so I could give my full attention to something without my left eye starting to twitch.

Some of the things I do to strengthen my ability to focus are things I've written about earlier: learning to be still in my room (stillness goes right for the jugular of distraction), muting my alarms and ringers (this doesn't kill all the distractions, but it wounds enough of them to let me get focused), and reflection time (contemplation requires concentration). When I practice holding focus I can control the distractions instead of being controlled by them.

While the snow globe helped me transition into my room, I found a timer helps me focus on my work. I'm not ashamed to admit this book would not have been written without a timer. Heck, it barely got written *with* a timer! It never fails when I sit down to work, I get called away or I think of four things I need to do that I'd forgotten about until just this moment. But early on, the timer kept me seated and focused on the task at hand for a certain period of time. I might quickly jot down the things that came to mind (I didn't want to forget them again!), but I stayed the course until the time was up.

When I first started using a timer, I set it for ten minutes. I wanted to be successful, and I knew if I set it for too long and didn't make it, I would feel like I couldn't do it or that I'd failed. During the ten minutes, I would give concentrated attention to whatever I was working on. I would turn off my email and put my phone on silent, but I wouldn't allow myself to get up for any reason (the children and blood excluded). And when my ten minutes was up, I would stop and take a little break. Now I'm up to over an hour at a time and I don't need to set the timer as much, but I still take little breaks for ten or twenty minutes before sitting back down to focus again.

Maybe you don't think concentrating for forty-five minutes or an hour is a long time. You might be surprised how hard it is to really pay attention to what you are paying attention to for that length of time. I did not know how difficult focusing would be until I started getting still. This revealed how much practice I needed to retrain my brain. My concentration is like a muscle that has become stronger with practice and repeated use.

While it's true that I can still be writing an email and decide to order something on Amazon, even that is getting more rare. I no longer have to settle for constant distraction. My twitching has almost stopped and I have fewer attention spans and one pretty good one. It is that one I'm trying to lengthen with practice.

A word about practice: Just a few years ago I decided

to take a calligraphy class. I'd wanted to for years, and because I'd freed up some space in my days, I was able to. I had a fantastic teacher who was one of those rare and fortunate people who could make a living doing what she loved to do. It was a great joy to take lessons from her.

More than the style or knowledge that I gained from the calligraphy class, it was her teaching on how to practice that left the greatest imprint on me. We would be in class for an hour and then she would assign us homework. No groans because she explained the importance of practicing these letters so that our hands and minds would get used to forming them. But the interesting thing to me was she wanted us to practice writing each letter only two times. I was still chewing on this when another student spoke up that she had already learned that "practice makes perfect" and she would do as many as it took to get them right. Our teacher paused and got very serious and said to her, "In my class you will follow the example I create and only practice writing it two times." We were all a little shocked by the sternness in her voice, and she added, "Practice doesn't make perfect, practice makes permanent." We sat silently taking in her words. "Perfect practice makes perfect. If you practice these letters incorrectly, you will learn them incorrectly.

I'd like you to follow the assignment I've asked you to do. Only create each letter two times until I check your work and make sure you're practicing correctly."

I will never forget her telling us that practice does not make perfect, practice makes permanent. Focusing our attention is not something we can achieve perfectly, like forming calligraphy letters. The important thing here is that practice makes permanent. If I regularly practice focusing my attention (or using any of the new ingredients I'm working on), it doesn't take long for it to become a habit. Creating good habits is the infrastructure that will support calm. Practicing these new ways will ensure they become permanent in our lives.

REDUCE: Multitasking

REPLACE WITH (AND PRACTICE): Working with My Hands

When I try to do multiple things at once, the myriad of things I'm trying to accomplish often don't get done as successfully as I'd like them to. Multitasking does not increase my productivity. Productivity increases productivity. Just as the hare discovered, speed does not always ensure you cross the finish line first. Or if you do cross first, but don't do the job well, speed counts for nothing. There is a reason fables like "The Tortoise and the Hare" are still around to teach us.

In my efforts to reduce and replace multitasking, I am increasing my quality control and even my quantity by slowing down and intentionally doing one thing at a time whenever possible. I will still make breakfast and lunches at the same time, but I will not try to phone my mother in the midst of it. I will often group similar tasks together to streamline them, like wait to pay bills until I'm going to pay them all, instead of paying one online while I'm waiting for my browser to load. But mostly, I am finding great success and joy in tackling one thing at a time, especially something I can use my hands to do that doesn't involve the computer.

I have a favorite dress-up necklace: a drop pendant with a delicate little chain. I don't wear it very often. Not only because I don't dress up that often but more because I never find myself with thirty extra minutes to get it untangled. Little jewelry gnomes live inside my jewelry box and throw raucous parties in there with their friends the raccoons. Any time I am in need of a specific necklace, I find they've been partying again.

Not long ago I had the extra time, and I chose to make the effort. I sat down with a needle and my glasses and worked on the little knots until they were all out. It took me almost an hour, but may I tell you, it was a spiritual experience. I could not have done this a couple of years ago. I would not have had the patience to sit with the necklace and get into the untangling without getting frustrated and giving up or knotting it up further. I realized after the fact that I was *not* multitasking. I was uni-tasking. I wasn't trying to make a grilled cheese and untangle my necklace while writing down items on the grocery list. I was doing one thing. Not one *more* thing. One thing only.

The interesting thing to me was how much I enjoyed it. I've found a new spiritual discipline—untangling necklaces. Sitting in my bedroom working on my necklace, I sat for almost an hour, with a couple of small interruptions, painstakingly getting the knots out, happy as a clam. I was engaged in an act of care for my necklace. I could have been making a grilled cheese sandwich, and if I had been doing only that, I could have embraced it in the same way, as an act of care.

But I also think it was calming because I wasn't trying to do three other things at the same time. I was paying attention to what I was doing with my hands and focusing on that. You can't rush untangling a necklace; that creates stress. *I have to get this darn thing untangled before I want to put it around someone's neck!* It is using my hands and not my brain that feels so calming.

I'm sure this is what people find so wonderful and

calming about gardening or needlework or even coloring or painting. I'm not a gardener or a painter, but I like calligraphy and I *love* to color. In fact, the rise of adult coloring books (a term which scared me at first) indicates how many other people find it calming to use their hands in a creative way. When I color with the kids, I find myself relaxing, and my mind gets a partial break, or at least switches to use a different set of circuits. I'm using my hands, not trying to write a dissertation. The pressure of thinking gives way to creating and creativity and calm ensues.

When was the last time you did something creative with your hands? Please don't tell me you are not crafty—I am the least crafty mother at my school. It isn't about crafty, it's about calm. It's about using your hands to get your mind off your brain. It doesn't even have to be artistic or creative. Here are some other ways I use my hands in order to bring calm to my spirit: I untangle things big and small. I write letters with pen and paper instead of on my computer. I water plants outside. I wrap presents artistically. I do needlework projects.

Many of these activities are ones I have embraced since The Day Life Fell Apart. Working with my hands doing *one* thing has become a source not only of calm but also of joy and care. These are not things anyone can do well from a place of anger, but interestingly enough, if I start to do something like color or needlework when I'm upset, my focus shifts off of my emotions and onto my hands. The activity itself creates calm and practicing makes it permanent.

REDUCE: Overcommitting

REPLACE WITH (AND PRACTICE): A Committed Promise

Those of us who love helping out and want to whenever possible always run the risk of volunteering, committing, agreeing to do more than we have time to do. I did it again tonight. I told someone I would do something on a timetable that was pretty much impossible for me. I set myself up for crazy, and not just myself, because my crazy affects my family. This is why there should be a support group for Overcommitters Anonymous. Could someone get working on this? I cannot start it, but I need to attend it. If you build it, I will come.

This is what I know to say and should have said tonight (feel free to memorize this if necessary). "I have a problem with overcommitting. My heart of 'want to' is bigger than my capacity to do so right now, so if possible, may I help instead by . . . ?" This statement will save lives, marriages, schools, and sanity! Instead of taking on the whole project, or even too much of it, I try to suggest something specific that I know I *can* do. "I can't host the party at my house, but I could coordinate the food or possibly send out the invitations."

The concept of reducing overcommitment is so much easier when replaced with a committed promise: "If it would benefit, I can help in this way instead." This simple statement allows me to be involved and actually help without taking on more than I can handle. It demonstrates my desire to help, but gives me the chance to do so in a way that is manageable. A committed promise also supports the relationship, and most people feel cared for and honored that you would suggest a creative way to be involved instead of closing the door with a no. No one is *ever* offended if you can offer more than you promised. But it can strain a relationship if you commit to too much and need to reduce your commitment.

So I am doing my best to reduce my tendency to overcommit by responding to requests with a committed promise instead. However, it helps me only when I actually do it. Funny how that works. When I don't practice this, I don't get better at managing my commitments and the idea of a committed promise remains in good idea land without doing any of the good.

REDUCE: Comparison

REPLACE WITH (AND PRACTICE): Gratitude and Generosity

My friend Dr. Curt Thompson, whom I've mentioned several times throughout these pages, is a psychiatrist. More than that, he is a man of great integrity, a mentor, a spiritual director, and the resident counselor for the Seasons Team. During one of our weekends, Curt said, "The brain cannot be anxious and grateful at the same time." *Whoa!* I remember as soon as he said it I grabbed my journal and scribbled it down.

He might as well have said, "The brain can't be crazy and calm at the same time!" This thought was like a seed planted that has grown into a strong hedge offering me protection against the negative comparisons I am prone to make in my mind: *Look* her *daughter's hair is combed. That woman must be a size two; she probably has a lot more time to work out. She and her husband seem like they talk about everything!* If I understood Curt right (and I believe I did because I came across a verse in the Bible that said basically the same thing [25]) then if, instead of making terrible comparisons that create thoughts that I'm not good enough, I choose to be grateful for what I have, the anxiety will go away. That is transformative. Want to reduce anxiety? Replace it with gratitude.

I try not to call things no-brainers around Curt, if

only because the brain is his life's work, but come on, this is so simple and so profound. Even a theater major like me can get it! When I have anxious thoughts that come from comparison and create anxiety, I can create calm by choosing to be grateful. So when I have thoughts like, *Look* her *daughter's hair is combed*, I can replace this negative thought with gratitude that I even have a daughter. Who cares about her hair? It was not a foregone conclusion I would have this amazing privilege and hair combed or not combed does not make one bit of difference—nor can I use it to make a statement about my worth as her mother. The minute I think about all I have to be grateful for, and my goodness I don't have to think long or hard, anxiety is banished and I feel humbled, deeply contented, and yes, "anxious for nothing."

I picture the feelings of gratitude like water in a well inside my heart. Whenever I pause to give thanks for what I have, the water level rises up inside the well. Whenever I'm feeling anxious, I can dip into the cool water of gratitude. But when I am ungrateful or if I lose touch with all I have to be grateful for, the water level in the well drops considerably. When I complain or grumble or compare myself to those I perceive as having it better than me, the well can actually dry up. I am sure there are some in whom the well has been dry so long it has crumbled into itself and become difficult to access. Fear and anxiety thrive in the absence of gratitude. They whisper lies such as, *If you give too much money, you won't have enough for yourself. You need this money. It's your money; when you make more, then you can be generous with it.* If we don't feel like we *are* enough, we seek to *have* enough to offset those feelings. Having the right house or car or purse will augment our worth in the eyes of others. But fear and anxiety create winds of discontent and bitterness that erode an already parched soul and not enough becomes never enough.

The water of gratitude changes everything; it is a wellspring of life. For me it is the way to drive a stake in the heart of comparison. Not only am I enough, what I have is more than enough, and I am grateful beyond measure for whatever it is as well as the chance to use it for the good of those around me and for the world.

If gratitude is like the water of the well in our hearts, generosity is that water of gratitude flowing out into the world. Generosity is when the gratitude in my heart spills out onto others. This water must keep flowing lest it grow stagnant inside us. Through generosity we release gratitude into the world. All the generous people I know are deeply and profoundly grateful for all they have been given. And every grateful person I know is generous with what they have. These are the happiest, most contented, calmest people on the planet. They are not riddled with anxiety or fear. They have deep wells of gratitude in their hearts that pump the water of life generously onto the parched ground around them.

I've been fortunate to get to meet many of these grateful and generous souls over the years. Quite surprising is how many of them are not what others would consider a person of means. They often explain that their gratitude and generosity did not come (as we might assume) when they had everything they wanted. In fact, it seems to me like it came the other way around. Gratitude and generosity only come when you want what it is that you have, regardless of how much or how little there is of it. This way of freedom is available to anyone willing to give thanks for what they have been given.

Replace comparison with gratitude; it is the path to less anxiety. Practice choosing gratitude to create life-giving water inside you, then watch it rise and overflow in generosity toward all.

REDUCE: Pressure
REPLACE WITH (AND PRACTICE): Laughter

A number of years ago, Roy and I went out on our date night. We were excited for a night under the stars at the Hollywood Bowl. The Bowl is an outdoor amphitheater with a reputation as the most wonderful place in all of Los Angeles to enjoy a concert. We packed a picnic dinner and blankets and settled in to listen to the LA Philharmonic in the cool of a California evening.

Slowly, I began to shed the cares of another busy week. We enjoyed dinner and were having dessert as I began to feel like a real person again, a grown-up, instead of just the mother of two little ones. I reminded myself, *This is why it is so important to go through the trauma of getting out for a night.* The sun had gone down and I wrapped one of the blankets around my shoulders as the orchestra made Mozart come alive. About halfway through the first piece, I heard a strange sound. It took me a little while to figure out what it was and where it was coming from, but once I discovered, I wished I hadn't.

The man sitting next to me was sucking his teeth. *This cannot be happening.*

I tried to focus my thoughts on something else. The music, the evening, anything but that horrible sound. *Please, God, help me tune this out. I don't get out much and I can't believe Mozart is going to be ruined by the teeth sucker sitting next to me.*

And then it came again. And again. And yes, again and still again. *Had it been roast beef? A turkey sandwich?*

What is so horribly lodged in that man's teeth that it still isn't out after twenty minutes of Mozart? Would it be rude to offer him a toothpick? Anything to salvage the evening.

Eventually, Roy and I switched places, and as luck would have it the man did not stay for the second half. We cheered, quietly of course, when he and his wife did not return to their seats after the intermission. I hoped he'd gone to buy dental floss!

Just a few nights ago we returned to the Hollywood Bowl. It had been at least six years since that experience, and as we told the friends with us about that evening, fresh fits of laughter interrupted the telling. Finally, some joy had come from that awful experience. It was so much funnier now. Looking back, I wish I could have laughed it off, but I was under too much pressure. It would have been just the thing to relieve the tension, but I couldn't get there. It was all I could do to keep from crying.

However, now, if Roy and I are in a tense situation, like stuck in traffic and he's about to blow a gasket, I can release the pressure in an instant simply by sucking my teeth.

I have a friend who quotes her grandmother as saying, "A day is wasted if we don't all fall over in a heap laughing." Laughter is a life-changing, life-giving, pressure-reducing gift, so unwrap it, open it up, and use it every chance you can. If we can't laugh, we'll spontaneously combust. Laughter is a release valve on the pressure cooker of life that keeps the temperature from getting too hot inside. When we take ourselves too seriously or find we're working too hard without breaks, the cure is laughter.

We all have a friend or two (or more if we're really lucky) who makes us laugh. Don't let them go on vacation or out of the country for any length of time—keep them very close. Maybe you're the funny one and you can make others laugh—never dismiss this gift. It is the best medicine there is for reducing the pressure of crazy.

One Tuesday morning, so much had gone wrong by nine o'clock that I felt like I was going to break down before breakfast (always a bad sign). I'd put the coffee on before bed (yay, me) but forgotten to empty the old coffee out of the stainless carafe, and I woke up to coffee all over the counter and floor. After cleaning up the mess, I went to get dressed in clothes I'd carefully laid out the night before (yay, me), but when I picked my bra up off the floor, the hook on the back snagged the carpet. I pulled out a whole row of carpet before I realized what was happening. A dryer sheet made a small fire that burned the load of whites I was trying to dry too quickly, and I received a summons for jury duty!

Thanks to Judith Viorst, I said out loud to no one, "And she could tell it was going to be a terrible, horrible, no good, very bad day!" Because even when you're trying to create calm in the center of crazy, some days are just like that, even in Santa Monica. I thought it was funny, so I called a friend to recount my mishaps, and we had a tears-running-down-your-cheeks laugh. All the pressure of a day that had started off so badly was released through the valve of laughter.

Then there was the afternoon I was driving home with Abigail from school. I was in my own world, probably feeling pressure over things that needed to get done when I got home. Abigail interrupted my thoughts with this sweet question, "Mommy, what were some things that you didn't have when you were little that we have now?" The question just melted my heart along with her interest, and I told her so. "That's a wonderful question, sweetie, let me think about it for a minute." I thought first about all the electronics, like iPods and iPads and smartphones, but I must have been taking too long to answer.

As if to help get me thinking, Abigail suggested, "Bricks?"

I snorted. I managed to keep the car on the road, but barely. "No, sweetheart, bricks were around when Mommy was a little girl." As I was still trying to recover from her suggestion that "bricks" were not around in the seventies, she offered the helpful follow-up, "How 'bout houses?" I didn't even try to hold it together. I was laughing so hard I could barely breathe, and Abigail was laughing too, but she had no idea what was so funny. A wonderful sense of joy filled the van, and I forgot whatever had been weighing on me, and we arrived home in such great spirits having laughed our heads off!

Want to reduce the stress in your life? Mine your stories. Remember things that made you laugh and use them again when things are tense. Write down incidents that happen as a family so you can recall them in pressure-filled situations. Laughter is dopamine-producing and enhances our sense of well-being by releasing endorphins and serotonin that make us feel good. Laughter is good medicine. Doctors practice medicine; we should practice laughter until it is permanent.

MY COMPLETE RECIPE FOR CREATING CALM

We've come full circle with this chapter. Here's a recap of the complete recipe for creating calm that I've shared in this book:

- Identify the top ingredients in your life that create crazy.

- If you're in a crisis, accept that it can be a catalyst to start your journey toward calm.
- Allow yourself to be held still by the safe, loving arms of God.
- Create a room of your own, a mental place of strength and beauty that can become a home for your soul.
- Sit still inside your room and spend time with yourself, even when it feels uncomfortable— especially when it feels uncomfortable.
- Do some homework to call all the pieces of yourself to the safety of "home."
- Using boundaries, set limits to things that create crazy in your life.
- Keep your Calm Keys handy and use them to unlock calm in your relationships.
- Replace old ingredients that create crazy with new ones that create calm. Keep your list of ingredients with your Calm Keys. Practice using them to make your changes permanent.

These are not the only ingredients out there for creating calm, far from it, but they are the specific ones that have helped me counter crazy. Your list will look different than mine and should include things that you enjoy and that you find counter the crazy and create calm. Write some of your ingredients down to remember them just like you do when there are items you need from the store. Keep your best items on hand and use them as often as possible.

WHAT KIND OF LIFE DO YOU WANT?

We choose the main ingredients that determine whether we will have a life of calm or a life of crazy. If we choose crazy ingredients, we get crazy outcomes. If we substitute calm ingredients, we will get a decidedly different result. Which means, we can create the life we want when we are intentional about choosing the best ingredients.

There is no limit to the choices we can make with regard to crazy and calm in our lives, but below are three short illustrations of different outcomes based on the ingredients selected.

A Crazy Life with a Crazy Center

The Williams family stocks the pantry with crazy-making items but does not admit to having a crazy life. Worse, they think their crazy life is normal. Their home is marked with regular chaos, demonstrated by fragmented, volatile relationships ("We are not speaking right now!"), high drama every day in mundane situations ("You would not believe what happened this time!"), and constant craziness instead of healthy consistency ("I know I said I would help you, but forgot I am supposed to pick up my mother from the airport and she will kill me if I'm late like I was last time!"). This kind of life, while crazy, would have been more acceptable had the Williamses not chosen to have three children. The Williams' kids are too young and too busy acting out to try to make sense of the crazy. But sometimes at night they wonder if life is supposed to be this way. The oldest Williams kid will likely become super responsible, growing up quickly to try to parent his parents, while the youngest girl will embody the crazy for a while, and then after rehab and therapy, she will struggle to find a new way to live differently than her parents did.

The Williamses' life looks crazy from the outside, and it pretty much is, because it is coming from the kind of crazy that never got examined from the inside.

A Calm Life with a Crazy Center

The Jackson-Malone family creates the appearance of a calm life, mostly through behavior control. They do not recognize the ways they create internal crazy, because everything looks so calm from the outside. Kinsey Jackson is uber-organized, impeccably dressed, and keeps her home looking like the model home they viewed before buying. Her family runs smoothly with labels, containers, and cubicles. As far as any observer can see, this family lives in a perfect and very calm world. Their only *real* problems are David Jackson's credit card debt, the eating disorder their daughter is hiding, and the way their dog tracks in dirt every time he goes outside. Kinsey didn't know the signs of anorexia, and when the doctor diagnosed her daughter, Kinsey ignored them at first because Jennifer was making good grades and staying in shape. Kinsey worries most about losing control. If she didn't shame her husband for his spending habits or take the dog for his bath once a week, there is no telling what could happen! Life would start crumbling like a gluten-free cookie. No, the reins must be held tight and all sugar locked up after school. No matter how much income David provides, the Jackson-Malone family will never feel like they have enough.

This family looks calm from the outside, but crazy is running rampant on the inside.

A Crazy Life with a Calm Center

The Harris family struggles with crazy circumstances and they have many challenges. The youngest Harris boy has special needs and relentless energy. Sarah often describes life as crazy, but she knows it's a characteristic of modern life and tries to roll with it. Sarah seeks to counter the craziness as she can, especially when she gets worn down. She finds relief through quiet walks and making time for coffee with friends who care for her. Sarah works to stay organized but doesn't obsess about clutter. Sarah and Kevin put more effort into repairing rips in relationships than in repairing rips in the furniture, even though Sarah would like to have the sofa recovered. She is careful with money but generous to those in need, believing there will always be enough to go around, even if that means sacrifice. Whether it's an extra person for dinner, an extra hundred dollars for a charity, or an extra day to volunteer, Sarah is grateful for all she's been given and feels joy in sharing it. The Harris family is not wealthy, but they know they have plenty. Kevin deeply appreciates his wife but assumes she knows this. He thinks his family is loud and too chaotic but knows the pitfalls of trying to control this. This family will spread out in proximity over the years after college, but they will remain close in relationship. Their children know how to care for each other by the example set by their parents.

The Harrises' life looks crazy to everyone on the outside. No one could imagine living their life with its challenges, but on the inside the Harris family experiences calm.

What kind of life do you want? Crazy or calm? This is the underlying question of this book, and if you can answer it honestly, you can have that life. If you want crazy, it's yours. You don't even have to do anything to create it; it will find you. In fact, crazy finds us the fastest when we do nothing. Crazy grows most rapidly when we aren't thinking about it and are just doing our best to get through the day without going postal.

On the other hand, if you want a life of calm, it is within your reach to create it. You do not have to wait until your circumstances calm down; they won't. You do not have to move to a deserted island with your children; you know you can't. This book suggests beginning with yourself on the inside and working your way out, not because this is the only way to calm, but because it was the way for me. I had to stop long enough to allow a home for calm to be created in my soul. It wasn't created on the go-between errands, nor was it created on vacation far away from home—calm was created right in the center of a very crazy life. I wrote this book so you would know if I could do it, you could too.

What kind of life do you want?

Conclusion

EVERY GIFT SHOP on every Main Street in every city, including Santa Monica, seems to stock some version of the saying, "Keep Calm and _____ On." It may be on a T-shirt or a plaque or a bumper sticker, but it will take some form like this:

- Keep Calm and Cupcake On
- Keep Calm and Coffee On
- Keep Calm and Have Another Glass of Wine

I see every variation possible. What I don't see much is the real statement: Keep Calm and Carry On.

Eight out of ten people (in my own tiny survey; okay, two of them were my kids) did not know where the statement comes from or what it means other than some cute way of saying have another cupcake and forget your troubles. Or, that in the case of emergency you should coffee on. Coffee is a verb now?

The saying is good for a laugh, but not so good for real life. It denies we live in a world with real pain and suffering that cupcakes don't solve. It makes light of the need to stay calm when the world is falling apart.

And it seems to me we've never needed calm more than we need it now. Since I began writing this book on creating calm, I have watched crazy multiply around me. Not crazy just as in busy, but crazy as in a friend's husband of ten years walking out the door, my parents having life-threatening illnesses, and a dear friend's daughter lost her vision. Last spring, my brother lost his job, another friend became homeless, and I had to spend multiple days in the hospital with diverticulitis. Keep calm and cupcake on? Give me a break! I take it back; I can't even laugh about it anymore.

Few will forget 2016 held the strangest, most contentious election any of us has ever seen. Regardless of your views on the outcome, America has now experienced crazy on the national level in ways we never imagined possible. Our country needs healing. Our people need hope for the future when life is hard and they cannot see what the future holds.

The original statement "Keep Calm and Carry On" came out of difficult times. In 1939 England was losing the Second World War. Winston Churchill was fighting for the free world against a maniacal dictator trying to overtake it. His country was coming apart at the seams.

The city of London was being bombed regularly setting off air-raid sirens in the middle of the night, causing terror, innocent people were dying in the streets, children were being sent away from their parents for reasons of safety, and the government was desperate to encourage its citizens to stay the course.

The government created a series of slogans to help get the word out to its citizens to stay strong. The slogans were printed and made into posters. Designed to boost morale they helped strengthen the resolve of a weary nation to keep fighting, even when its citizens couldn't fully comprehend what they were fighting for. The posters were tacked up all over London and into the countryside and anywhere else they could be posted. The most famous of these slogans was "Keep Calm and Carry On."

This simple statement quite possibly separated the living from the dying. There may come a time in our own nation when those who know how to carry on calmly will be the only ones able to counter the crazy. If history is any teacher, the greatest danger always comes from the crazy that refuses to recognize how crazy it really is.

I hope we meet and yet I hope we never run into each other in the grocery store. There are days I am doing this so imperfectly I wish I had written someone else's name down as the author of this book. My name is on it because this is the story of my own journey, from crazy to less crazy, otherwise known as calm. It has been a messy trip, full of pain, disappointments, and some ugly realizations about myself, but it has also been a joyful trek that has held God moments, surprises, and the best gift of all: Coming *home* to myself.

The people who inspire me most do not have it all or have it all together. People who say they do, or put forth that image, really don't—trust me on this. And if by any chance you meet a person who does seem to have it all together, usually that person would be shocked you think they do. Those who inspire me are the ones who can *hold* things together honestly or let things fall apart, because they know who they are despite the outcome of their circumstances.

So let's join our resistance movements together. It shouldn't be too difficult to find each other if we try. We will not be the ones striving to keep life neat and tidy or the ones stressing about balance. We will not be the ones scurrying breathlessly to every event and meeting, spending more time rushing than a running back in the NFL. We will not be the ones giving in to fear, afraid of saying no or of setting limits to crazymakers—people who try to monopolize our time or shame us into commitments. We will not be the ones constantly derailed by the unhealthy, crazy way others around us might be choosing to live.

We'll be the ones looking into the faces of others while we converse, focused and attentive, resisting the urge to check our phones. We'll be the ones who make other people wonder why we have so much freedom to stay calm. We'll be the ones seeking to tell the whole truth about our struggles, especially when they are the hardest. We'll be the ones staying home a little more to kick FOMO in the teeth and add more structure to our calm. We'll be the ones unwilling to settle for distracted, overcommitted, chaotic, crazy lives. We'll be the ones creating calm in the center of all kinds of crazy.

My guess is that it will be pretty easy to find each other.

Acknowledgments

"EVEN A BLIND SQUIRREL finds an acorn some-times." This is not a statement of false humility, nor is it to imply that anyone I want to thank here is a nut. This is a simple metaphor that expresses the way I feel about the bounty that has supported me in my life and work. In my stumbling, often foolish attempts to create anything—a book, a drama, a weekend experience—I have come across some incredible human "acorns." So many that to take the credit for whatever has been accomplished would be sheer hubris on my part. The acclaim I will accept is being wise enough to gather up these remarkable people when I have come across them.

Zondervan, thank you for taking a chance on an author who hasn't written a book in nine years. Your belief in me as a writer empowered me to press on despite unforeseeable obstacles and delays. Thank you for your understanding and patience. It is the rare and blessed author who feels valued as a person, not just a project.

Carolyn McCready, I feel sorry for any author who doesn't get to work with you, and slightly guilty that

I do. You made a difficult process (I won't say easy, because you care so much) considerably less difficult than it has always been. While it has been a privilege to be your friend all these years, it is a dream come true to work with you.

Liz Heaney, you've made me a better writer and, through that process, a better person. Your skills and training got me back into writing shape. This book would not have come to be without your editorial care, and if by chance it had, only three people would have liked it.

Convoy of Hope, thank you for the opportunity to make a difference in this world in a way I never imagined I could. Your efforts in empowering women all over the world make God smile. (And them too!)

Dr. Ryan Davis and the Mind Health Institute, your work is creating calm by restoring the dignity and joy stolen by mental illness and the traumas of life. Powerful.

To the parent community at SAE, thank you for your constant support regardless of the fluctuating level of my participation. But, see? I really was writing. Stephanie, our walks and talks in the mornings after drop-off breathed fresh life into this manuscript.

My dear Seasons Team, not only have you influenced the content of this book, you have changed the trajectory of my life. Our weekends together have been transformative for so many, but none that needed it more than me. Curt, Jay, Katherine, Pepper, Noah, Amy, Melissa, Shanelle, Brook, Terry, this squirrel hit the mother lode the day we all came together. I found you and you found me and our voyage into the deep continues.

Wendy, Linda, Susan, Shirley, Jill, David and Ellen, Dick and Marvel, and the broader Seasons Weekend community of participants, thank you for coming alongside us with your time, money, and willingness to do the hard work of spiritual transformation in community. You inspire me in the ways you are bringing calm to the inside and outside crazy in your own lives. I'm grateful to be on this journey with friends like you.

Pepper Sweeney, your genius has been the secret ingredient in my dramatic work for almost two decades. Now the secret is out. Please return my call.

The one and only Amy Cella, after sixteen years we are living with less crazy than ever before. If anything ever happens to me, you know what to do—just not sure I would know what to do if anything happened to you. So let's avoid that.

Wendy, I couldn't know how much I needed you when I stumbled across your path, but I'm a quick learner. I give thanks every day for your friendship and support, for me and for Seasons.

Angela, my lifelong friend, we have been through more together over a few years than some have had to go through in a lifetime. I couldn't have found a better friend if I'd been a squirrel able to see. God knows his acorns well and in whose path to put them.

Mom and Dad, you continue to inspire me with a love that seems to grow every day. Mom, thank you for encouraging me to share my full story, even though some parts are still quite painful. Dad, you are the most patient caregiver I have ever had the privilege to see up close. Your sacrifice and care for Mom is a magnificent thing of beauty. You are building a great cathedral and I want you to know I see it.

Roy, Elliot, and Abigail, you are the three best reasons in the whole world to create calm. Your love and support for me in the writing of this book were nothing short of sacrificial. Abigail, even though this book didn't end up needing pictures, I've loved every drawing you created and have kept them in my book file. Elliot, your heart is passionate and true and I couldn't be more proud of you. Roy, we got a late start, but we're finishing well. Your love and care have given me the deepest gift imaginable: a home like I've never known.

Notes

1. C. S. Lewis, *The Problem of Pain* (1940; San Francisco: Harper, 2001), 91.
2. "Stress Effects on the Body," American Psychological Association, http://www.apa.org/helpcenter/stress-body .aspx.
3. Kathleen Norris, *Acedia and Me: A Marriage, Monks, and a Writer's Life* (New York: Penguin, 2008), 74.
4. Psalm 42:3 NIV.
5. "Leading Causes of Death in Females," Centers for Disease Control and Prevention, http://www.cdc.gov/ women/lcod/.
6. "Women and Heart Disease Facts," Women's Heart Foundation, http://www.womensheart.org/content/ heartdisease/heart_disease_facts.asp.
7. QBQ!, http://qbq.com.
8. Bruce Springsteen, interview by Ted Koppel, *Nightline Up Close*, ABC News (October 2, 2002).
9. Cat Stevens, "The First Cut Is the Deepest," *New Masters*, Polydor, 1967.
10. Anne Lamott's Facebook page, https://www.facebook .com/AnneLamott, accessed October 16, 2016.
11. After the Rescue, "You Love Me Still," *After the Rescue*.

By writer Noah Needleman. Performed by After the Rescue. Producer Noah Needleman, 2016. CD/MP3.

12. Edith Wharton, *The Touchstone*.

13. Peter Kreeft, *Christianity for Modern Pagans* (San Francisco: Ignatius, 1993), 172.

14. First published on October 24, 1929, the essay was based on a series of lectures she delivered at Newnham College and Girton College, two women's colleges at Cambridge University in October 1928.

15. Teddy Wayne, "The End of Reflection," *New York Times* (June 11, 2016), http://www.nytimes.com/2016/06/12/fashion/internet-technology-phones-introspection.html?_r=0.

16. Curt Thompson, *Anatomy of the Soul: Surprising Connections between Neuroscience and Spiritual Practices That Can Transform Your Life and Relationships* (Carol Stream, Ill.: Tyndale, 2010), 195.

17. Fr. Richard Rohr, "Nonviolence: Weekly Summary," Center for Action and Contemplation, https://cac.org/category/daily-meditations/2016/10/.

18. Kreeft, *Christianity for Modern Pagans*, 168.

19. Arthur Bennett, ed., *The Valley of Vision: A Collection of Puritan Prayers and Devotions* (Edinburgh: Banner of Truth Trust, 1975).

20. Dennis Hamm, SJ, "Rummaging for God: Praying Backwards through Your Day," *IgnatianSpirituality.com*, http://www.ignatianspirituality.com/ignatian-prayer/the-examen/rummaging-for-god-praying-backward

-through-your-day. Reprinted from *America*, May 14, 1994, with permission of America Press, Inc. ©1994.

21. Kreeft, *Christianity for Modern Pagans*, 124.

22. K. F. W. Wander, *Deutsches Sprichwörter-Lexikon* (German Dictionary of Proverbs), vol. 4, (1876). The proverb is contained with a short explanation but without source.

23. Amit Chowdhry, "Research Links Heavy Facebook and Social Media Usage to Depression," *Forbes* (April 30, 2016), http://www.forbes.com/sites/amitchowdhry/2016/04/30/study-links-heavy-facebook-and-social-media-usage-to-depression/#60353ff07e4b.

24. Dr. Ryan Davis, Mind Health Institute, Beverly Hills, California, www.mhi-bh.com.

25. Philippians 4:6–7 NIV.

FOR MORE INFORMATION or to download free discussion questions for *Creating Calm in the Center of Crazy*, please visit:

WWW.CREATINGCALMINTHECENTEROFCRAZY.COM

For more information about Nicole Johnson's speaking or dramatic presentations, please visit:

WWW.NICOLEJOHNSON.ORG

Seasons is a nonprofit organization created to facilitate personal and transformative experiences with God in the context of community. For more information about Seasons Weekends, please contact:

WWW.SEASONSWEEKEND.COM

SEASONS, INC.
212 26th Street #204
Santa Monica, CA 90402
310-899-0099